Creative
Rug Hooking

Anne D. Mather

Sterling Publishing Co., Inc.
NEW YORK

PHOTOGRAPHERS:
Ron Lindahn, Valhalla Studio, Rabun Gap, Ga.; and Anne Mather

ARTISTS:
Gail Loder and Tom Mather

LETTERING CHAPTER
extracted from Pris Buttler's pamphlet, "Lettering Tips for the Rug Hooker"
(Pris Buttler Rug Designs, 2000)

Book design by Richard Oriolo
Edited by Claire Bazinet

Library of Congress Cataloging-in-Publication Data
Mather, Anne D.
    Creative rug hooking / Anne D. Mather.
      p. cm.
    ISBN 0-8069-7146-0
    1. Rugs, Hooked. 2. Rugs Hooked—Patterns. I. Title

TT850.M395 2000
746.7'4—dc21   00-030132

1 3 5 7 9 10 8 6 4 2

Published by Sterling Publishing Company, Inc.
387 Park Avenue South, New York, N.Y. 10016
© 2000 by Anne D. Mather
Distributed in Canada by Sterling Publishing, c/o Canadian Manda Group,
One Atlantic Avenue, Suite 105, Toronto, Ontario, Canada M6K 3E7
Distributed in Great Britain and Europe by Cassell PLC
Wellington House, 125 Strand, London WC2R 0BB, England
Distributed in Australia by Capricorn Link (Australia) Pty Ltd., P.O. Box 6651,
Baulkham Hills, Business Centre, NSW 2153, Australia
Printed in Hong Kong
Sterling ISBN 0-8069-7146-0

To Katherine Skogstad Lord

Acknowledgments

Mary Williamson served as my content editor, key resource, and top fact-checker on this book as well as *The Art of Rug Hooking*; her advice and support were indispensable. Martha Morris was an invaluable resource. She opened up her home and heart to me, sharing years of rug-hooking wisdom. The members of my writing group deserve special thanks for their forthright but always supportive criticism: Thank you, Kathy Barnes, Dawn Clutter, Jack Curtis, Jean Hendrick, Claire Karssiens, and Fritzie Seifert, and emeritus members Rod and Carol Houghton, Regina McIntyre, and Ted Slautterback. Rug hookers around the country were so generous with their time and talents to make this book happen; special thanks to the 50 represented here, plus designers Patsy Becker, Barbara Brown (Port Primitives), Pris Buttler (Pris Buttler Rug Designs), Sue Hamer, Bett McLean, Sandy Myers, Charlotte Price (Charco Patterns), Margaret Siano (Lib Callaway Patterns), and Jeanette Szatkowski (Harry M. Fraser Co.). I am grateful to Alice Berg of Little Quilts, who suggested the theme for this book. Special thanks to my husband, Brian, who is always so supportive of my "positive addictions," and to our lovely daughters, Maggie and Jeannie. Finally, a special thanks to my Sterling editor Claire Bazinet and book designer Richard Oriolo.

Ambrosia

Hooked by Margaret Howell. Designed by Jane McGown Flynn.
SIZE: 44 by 72 inches

Contents

Rug Hooking:
The Secret of Style

Jim Dandy's Kingdom

Designed and hooked by Mary Mann.

SIZE: 34.5 by 37.5 inches

Your art is a secret

You are ready to tell.

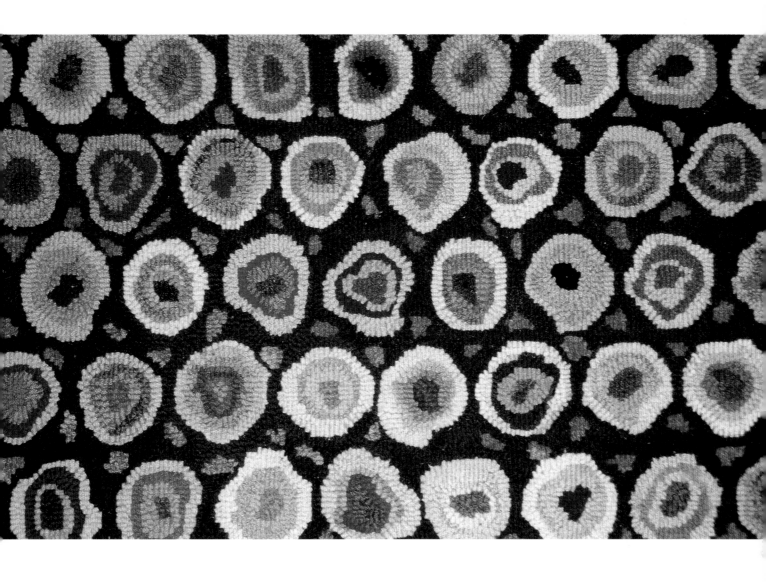

Cat's Paw *(close-up)*

Hooked by Pat Stolberg. Designed by Pearl K. McGown (Joan Moshimer's Rug Hooker Studio).
SIZE: 37 by 55 inches

You have themes to your life
And your art.
Circles.

Paper Doll Rug

Two variations hooked and designed by Anne Mather.
SIZE: 23.5 by 25 inches (top); 21.5 by 33 inches (bottom)

Lessons that bear repeating,

Joys that never stop giving.

Like children.

Molly

Hooked and designed by Pam Wiegand. SIZE: 36.5 by 28 inches

But that's the part you know.
The flags you wave,
The songs you sing.

King's Pottery Face Jug Rug

Hooked and designed by Anna King. SIZE: 28.5 by 27 inches

There is more.

Spiritual addictions.

Abram's Creek Stag

Hooked by Anne Mather. Designed by Bett McLean. SIZE: 53 by 53 inches

The compulsion to create certain subjects.

Twinkle Stars

Hooked by Patty Moskoff. Designed by Kathy Morton (Morton House Primitives).
SIZE: 18.5 by 24 inches

Patterns, perhaps.

Read Me a Rhyme

Hooked by Pat Chancey. Designed by Flo Petruchik. SIZE: 26 by 40 inches

Childhood tales

You haven't thought of in years.

Stella Hay Rex

Hooked by Martha Morris. Designed by Stella Hay Rex (Margaret Siano, Hook Nook).
SIZE: 43 by 72 inches

And flowers, always:
Peonies and pansies
Pedulas, when in doubt.

Woodland Adventure (close-ups below)

Hooked and designed by Trudy DuVerger. SIZE: 28 by 42 inches (first rug)

And, of course, animals.

Uncle Wiggily

Hooked by Marguerite Culberson. Adapted from *Uncle Wiggily And His Friends* by
Howard R. Garis (1939); copyright 1996 by Uncle Wiggily Classics, Amherst, Massachusetts.
SIZE: 38 by 29.5 inches

You are haunted by these subjects
But do not know why.

Scrap Cats

Hooked by Katie Puckett and Judy Colley. Designed by Judy Colley. SIZE: 73 by 39 inches

Only that you are deeply satisfied
By creating them
Again and again
On your burlap.

The Cavalier

Hooked by Maryon Clonts. Based on a 14th-century tapestry, *The Cavalier*, the original of which hangs in a museum in Siena, Italy. SIZE: 42 by 54 inches

And colors.
What draws you
Again and again
To certain hues?

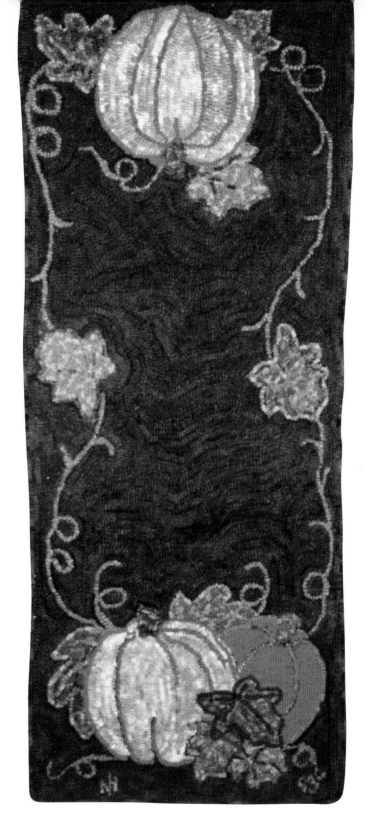

Pumpkins

Hooked and designed by Nancy Hackney. SIZE: 35 by 15 inches

To bronze greens.

Reddy Fox

Hooked by Dot Schutte. Designed by Jane McGown Flynn (Charco Patterns).
SIZE: 20.5 by 16 inches

Silver grays.

Hive with Vines

Hooked by Anne Mather. Designed by Bett McLean. From the collection of Janet Denlinger.
SIZE: 23.5 by 34 inches

Reds as ripe as raspberries.

The Whole Week's Pickings

Hooked by Barbara Moran. Designed by Pris Buttler. SIZE: 23.5 by 31 inches

Your palate may be subtle and subdued.

Caesar

Hooked by Sarah Owens. Based on an 1876 oil canvas, *Prize Bull,* by H. Call, in the National
Art Gallery, Washington, D.C. SIZE: 23 by 34 inches

Or wild and whimsical.

C a r i b *(close-up)*

Hooked by B. J. Andreas. Designed by Jane McGown Flynn (Charco Patterns).
SIZE (entire rug): 30 by 56 inches.

Or change from rug to rug.
Either way, it is more passion than choice:
Not to be denied.

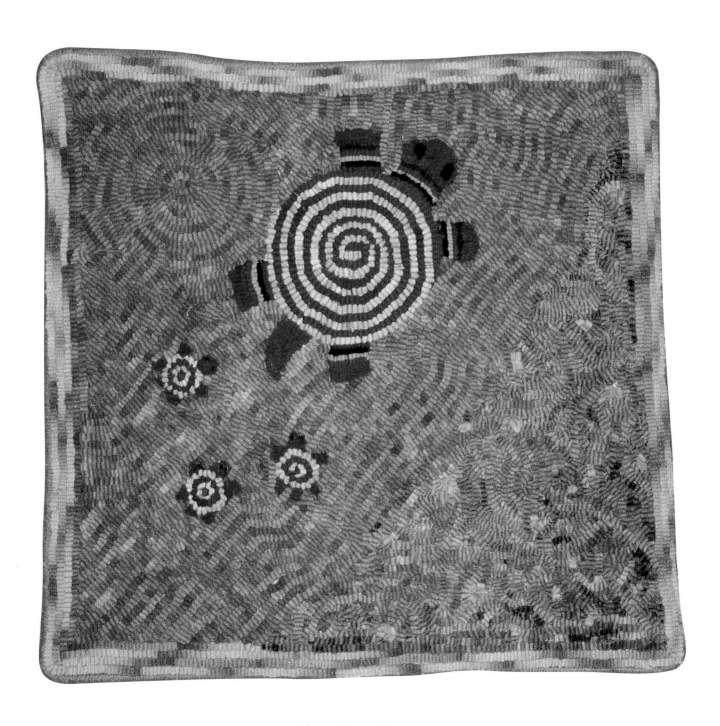

This Way Home

Hooked and designed by Carol Houghton. SIZE: 16.5 by 17 inches (first rug)

Your style is your art.

The essence of what you know...

Le Château
Hooked and designed by Eric Sandberg. Based on a 19th-century French painting. (Pattern available through Charco Patterns.) SIZE: 19 by 25 inches

The innocence of what you don't know…
And would like to know.

Tennessee Contentment

Hooked and designed by Mary Paul Wright. SIZE: 31 by 52 inches

Here you can be architect and archivist.
Color landscapes in tweeds, mountains in plaids
And lakes in the blue you would have them be.

Adam and Eve

Hooked by Anne Mather. Designed by Barbara Brown (Port Primitives). SIZE: 18 by 25 inches

Put Caribbean poppies
In your Garden of Eden.

Vineyard Chicks

Hooked by Anne Mather. Designed by Barbara Brown (Port Primitives). SIZE: 24 by 33 inches

Strew candy corn
For your fanciful fowl.

Tree of Bethlehem *(close-up inset)*

Hooked by Mary Williamson. Designed by Margaret Masters (Prairie Craft House).
SIZE: 37 by 33 inches

Reveal mysteries and yearnings.

Unspoken.

Perhaps even to yourself.

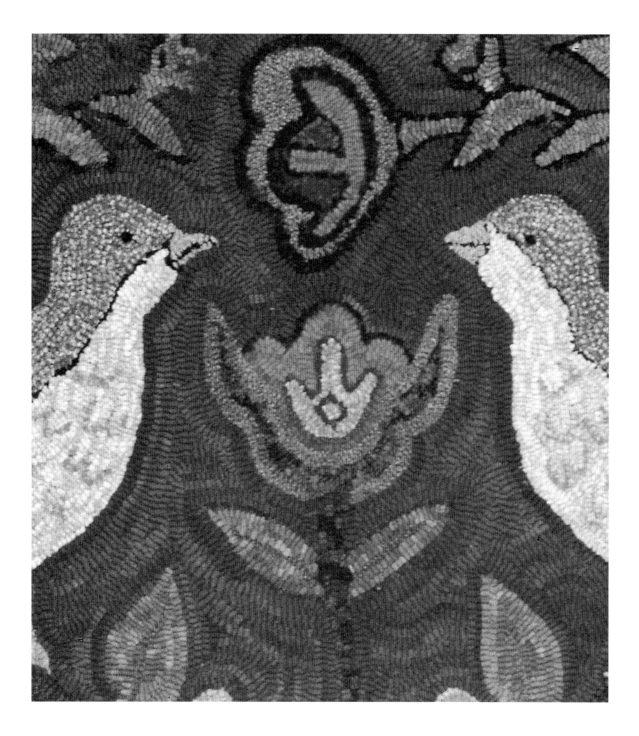

B and B (close-up)

Hooked by Barbara Moran. Designed by Patsy Becker. SIZE (entire rug): 32 by 42 inches

Your rug becomes a secret
You are ready to tell.

Making Patterns
Personal

Primitive rugs, such as Sarah Owens's original *The Girls*, are especially popular today.

"Let the beauty we love be what we do."
—RUMI

Rug Hooking:
The "Forgiving" Art

Rug hooking—creating rugs with strips of woolen fabric pulled through a fabric such as linen or burlap—is an ancient art, but one that had a particular hold on 19th-century America. Turning cast-off clothing into useful, artistic pieces appealed to our forebears, much as quilting did; indeed these "companion" crafts were once equally popular.

Today, rug hooking's appeal is again on the rise—and not just as a craft but to collectors. America, Australia, Canada, and England are all exhibiting a renewed interest in this fiber art. There are numerous reasons for this renaissance. One is the need to balance our increasingly technological lives with a sensual, creative pursuit. Like woodworking—which is now the number-one craft in America—hooking engages our hands and challenges our senses. And like the feel of a smooth, newly milled piece of wood, the variety of texture we can hook with—tweeds, herringbones, flannels—speaks to us in some primitive, soul-satisfying way.

Rug hooking is also relatively simple to learn, as needlework goes. Basically, it consists of one stitch—pulling a loop of wool through a hole. So, very soon after learning this art, the hooker's hands are engaged in that happy, "hypnotic luxury of repeated stitches" that is so inexplicably soothing to a frazzled spirit.

This art is also "so companionable," as veteran hooker and designer Martha Morris said to me. You can do it with your family. Or, like quilters, you can gather in klatches, sharing support and stories. Throughout the country, fabric artists are meeting in weekly or monthly groups, not to mention week-long rug camps, where they hook and form friendships to their hearts' content. This is a major catalyst to the growth of this craft—and one of its true blessings.

Rug hooking also entices us into the world of color. Many believe, in fact, that of the four elements of hooking—technique, design, texture, and color—the last is the most important. Certainly, it is what grabs us first about a rug, or a piece of fabric. Rug hooking is an excuse for every fabric lover to go wild—simply for the pleasure that color and texture give us. And because most of us are involved in color and fabric choices in so many ways in our lives—from shopping for clothes for ourselves and our families to decorating our homes with drapes and upholstery—this very artistic element of hooking comes with an ease that is surprisingly natural.

Which leads me to another reason I think this fiber art is mushrooming: it makes us look good. Or rather, we are good at it. Except when hooking orientals and certain tapestries, this is not a craft that requires you to draw precisely. Crudely drawn figures on a primitive rug are not embarrassing, just more endearing: any vintage primitive rug will illustrate that. And if you just can't seem to get your loops even, you have created more texture, and often a certain naiveté that is all the more charming. Moreover,

by the time your rug has been blocked and walked on a bit, no one will notice the difference. In a word, rug hooking is a very *forgiving* fiber art.

You will love your very first piece. I guarantee it. And to prove it, I have included several "first rugs" in this book (including my own). Several hookers featured in this book have been hooking for less than one year. Indeed, with a few notable exceptions, this book deliberately features the work of mostly unknown hookers. The take-home message, I hope, is clear: You can do this. You can do it creatively and uniquely.

There is yet a final reason the craft is so appealing—perhaps the ultimate one. It may make the beginner look good, but it still challenges the expert. There are many levels to rug hooking. Once you have mastered technique, you have the whole world of color planning—learning how colors complement, fight, and play off each other—to explore. You can also design your own rugs—or ones for others.

Like pottery, hooked rugs can be collectibles.

And, finally, you can learn to dye. Each of these areas is an art unto itself and probably a factor that draws artists from other media (oils, pastels) to rug hooking. It can require enormous skill and color sense. Rug hooking may be easy to learn, but you can spend a lifetime mastering it.

If you are totally new to this craft, the basic stitch and some general rules are given at the back of this book. I will also walk you through the creation of your own personal *Paper Doll Rug,* featuring a child in your life, and provide numerous other hooking projects and patterns—including new ones by Barbara Brown (Port House Primitives), Sue Hamer, Sandy Myers, Gail Loder, and myself. Plus we've included beloved favorites by Patsy Becker, Lib Callaway, Pat Hornafius (Fraser), Bett McLean, and Jane McGown Flynn.

Other rug hookers and I will illustrate and share techniques for hooking children, animals, houses, borders, and story rugs. Pris Buttler—an award-winning folk artist and rug designer—has contributed an entire section on how to letter, and we've also included several sample alphabets.

For more details on hooking, color planning, and dyeing, you may want to refer to my first book, *The Art of Rug Hooking* (Sterling, 1998).

The author's first rug—an adaptation of a Pat Hornafius pattern, *Renfrew Cats*— illustrates the charm of even a poorly executed primitive rug.

Developing
Your Own Style

The concept of personalizing your rug hooking may seem almost redundant, for surely this is the most individualized of the fiber arts. Often, we have no commercial pattern. Even when we do use one, we can—and often do—change it. Our patterns do not arrive color-coded, nor do local craft shops carry trays and trays of specially dyed woolens for our every need. No, we hookers are pretty much on our own with our art, and that's the way we like it.

"This is not hook by number," Illinois rug-hooking teacher Sue Hamer says. Even similar or identical patterns will appear vastly different when executed by different hookers, as the two versions of Adam and Eve opposite illustrate. Colors vary, as do textures and techniques. And in these rugs the devil is in the details—for sure! Note how both rugs richly embellish the devilish form, yet so differently: a paisley diamond style in one, lime-colored and gold stripes in the other. And what a difference in mood the choice of background colors makes.

Even when the color choices in a rug would seem fairly predictable—as in patriotic themes, for example—the style of the artist dominates. For example, look at Marilyn Bottjer's *Stars and Stripes* and Pat Tritt's *Sam, Sam, Sam* on page 42. Each basically employs reds, whites, and blues. But the similarity stops there. Marilyn's style incorporates subtle spot-dyeing, shading, and a sophisticated background technique. Pat's rug is more primitive, with an almost abstract, painted border.

What differentiates each of these rugs is the hooker's style. Defining style is a little like defining art, which is daunting, to say the least. My favorite definition of poetry is Carl Sandburg's "the synthesis of hyacinths and biscuits." What a lovely description for rug hooking as well: taking the ordinary (the fabric, the familiar in

Even similar patterns look vastly different when executed by different hookers. Above, Anne Mather's version of Port Primitive's *Adam and Eve*; below, Anna King's version of Patsy Becker's pattern, *Love Apple*.

(Above) Pat Tritt's original, *Sam, Sam, Sam.* (Right) Marilyn Bottjer's *Stars and Stripes* (pattern: Harry M. Fraser).

our lives, the "biscuits") and the extraordinary ("hyacinths") and merging them to mysteriously create art.

For me, style is authenticity. It's being yourself in the creating of your rug, flaws and all. It's using the colors you can't walk out of a store without buying…using the width of wool that just feels good in your hands…creating what *you* want to exist. In a word, it's bringing *yourself* to a rug. And when you do this, you're authentic, whether you create your own patterns or adapt those of others.

> *"Once you buy your pattern, it is yours*
> *to alter in any way you please.*
> *Make it a 'one of a kind.'"*
>
> —MARTHA MORRIS

Adapting Existing Patterns

Most rug hookers who use a pattern alter it. There are two main ways to do this: by deleting something or by adding something.

Deletions: "Editing" a Rug

I make my living as a writer and editor. I learned, while writing my first book, that when a certain line or paragraph just didn't work—when I kept working it over, fiddling with it, massaging it to get it to say what I wanted to say—it was best to just take it out altogether. Amazingly, I found I rarely missed what wasn't there. The resistance I was getting was a signal that, for some reason, that thought didn't belong there. I use this principle constantly in editing and writing.

So when I began rug hooking, I naturally followed the same editing pattern. If I hooked a blue spruce two or three times and it still kept looking strange to me, instead of continuing to "fix" it, I just removed the tree and, voilà! I was happier, the rug looked better, and it was easier! Now this is part of *my* style: I prune and simplify by nature. So I am happiest with those rugs that I "edit" to suit my taste. In the two versions, then, of *Vineyard Chicks* you'll find on the next page, you can probably readily decipher which one is mine—the one with much less detail. I took out the leaves and several tendrils. (I also changed the row of bricks into candy corn.) The other artist, Ruth Reenstra, on the other hand, kept these details, and her rug is all the richer for it. The take-home lesson is: Let your rug express what *you* want it to.

Another example of this principle is *Endearing Elegance*, Pris Buttler's tribute to women's friendship. Judy Colley's beautiful example includes almost all of the details that folk-artist Buttler incorporated into her original pattern. Mary

Two versions of the same rug—*Vineyard Chicks* by Port Primitives—illustrate personalized rug hooking.
Above, hooked by Anne Mather; below, by Ruth Reenstra.

Williamson edited out many of these—the drapes, the stacked books, the candlesticks, the flowers in the border—in her version. Again, each rug is gorgeous—and unique.

So some hookers delete details, naturally making patterns less "busy." By contrast, other hookers often add things to their rugs: butterflies, bumblebees, crows, twig borders, lettering, whatever; and the results are charming, personal, one of a kind.

Authenticity. The law of least effort. Whatever you want to call it, when you hook in a way that feels natural, the rug will flow smoothly. If you fight your instincts, the hooking turns into work. And then, I think, it loses its spark, its artistry.

When I ran this theory by my Cherokee healer (and rug-hooking) friend Carol Houghton, she instantly agreed. "When Cherokee feel resistance, we turn in a circle until we feel the place of ease; that's the place we go, rather than pushing against the resistance," she said. I think that we are most artistic as rug hookers when we find *our* place of ease.

Making Additions, Substitutions

One rug hooker who just can't leave a pattern alone is Martha Morris, an elegant, quiet-spoken veteran of the rug-hooking world who now lives in Gainesville, Georgia. Rug hooking should be personal, Martha maintains. She should know. She has been hooking for the past three decades and been

"privileged to know or learn from," as she puts it, such rug-hooking "greats" as Alice Beatty, Stella Hay Rex, Pearl McGown, Joan Moshimer, Connie Charleson, Happy DiFranza, Jean Armstrong, Anne Ashworth, Elizabeth Black, and Jule Marie Smith. Not to mention her dear friend Lib Callaway ("the 'mother' of primitive rug hooking"),

Two versions of Pris Buttler's pattern *Endearing Elegance*, by Judy Colley (above) and Mary Williamson (below). Note how Williamson's version "edited out" many details.

A rug hooker's version of wall-to-wall carpeting is illustrated in the Gainesville home of Martha Morris.

with whom she scouted out—and drew off—many an old primitive pattern.

In that time, Martha has created some seventy rugs, most from patterns—and she's changed almost every one of them. One gets the sense that this is not

only her artistic prerogative (she was an art minor in college and has made dolls and samplers, done petit point and oil painting before turning to rug hooking). Rather, changing patterns is for Martha an imperative, almost a necessity. She

actually needs, as she puts it, to make each rug "one of a kind."

On the simplest level, Martha does this by following a pattern but fleshing it out with rich details. Take DiFranza's *The Lion*, for example. Shown is an example of the lion's face, as drawn on the pattern. It is stark, devoid of shadow and of all but the outlines of features. In short, it is a typical rug-hooking pattern. Now, note Martha's hooked version. The difference is in the details.

Another example of detailing a pattern is shown in Martha's version of Pris Buttler's pattern, *The Christmas Three*. In the original pattern, none of the cen-

Close-ups of (above left) DiFranza's pattern, *The Lion*, unhooked; (right) as hooked by Martha Morris. (Below) *The Christmas Three*, hooked by Martha Morris, designed by Pris Buttler.

Martha Morris's *Cape Cod* (top), created by significantly altering the Lib Callaway pattern, *The Village* (below).

tral figures—the angel, snowman, or Santa—has any facial features, something Martha had to change. "When something's that cute, you've just got to make it pretty," she explains.

This technique—creating details

through shading, directional hooking, highlights, and addition of detail—is the very "stuff" of rug hooking, and most experienced hookers do it to some degree—some more than others.

However, in other rugs, Martha goes

a step further—actually replacing parts of a rug with something more to her liking, or adding new elements altogether. Take, for example, her large rug *Cape Cod*. This started with Lib Callaway's pattern, *The Village*, a much smaller (30-by 58-inch) rug. Martha personalized it by adding pieces of her genealogic past: a family residence, the Cape, a lighthouse, and family names printed out on the border. She also added the *Mayflower* in the background, an inlet for balance in the right corner, and a flag. Finally, she muted the background, hooking it in colors similar to the road that transects the pattern so that it does not dominate the rug. Similarly, she fleshed out the pattern's original "bony" trees into full, lush ones. The result: a totally unique rug.

Personalized details from Martha Morris's *Cape Cod* rug.

Martha Morris changed Lib Callaway's pattern, *The Grape Arbor*, by adding a lettered border and many animals, symbols of her family members.

Another example of changing a rug by adding to it is illustrated above in Martha's version of Lib Callaway's *The Grape Arbor*. The central folk-art motif of a young woman sitting under a grape arbor constitutes the original rug. All of the animals—symbolic of members of her family—and the wonderful lettered border (taken from an old sampler) were Martha's additions.

Creating themed borders is a good way for someone who has never created her own pattern to "get her feet wet."

Adapting Borders

Borders are the "frames" of a rug. And the most traditional rug borders resemble frames: 1 to 3 inches of solid or variegated color, dark enough to "set off" the central design. The border is an area that many hookers alter to make their rug more personal. In addition to the lettered border, such as Martha Morris introduced opposite in *The Grape Arbor* (and which will be explored in detail in our section on lettering), hookers use many other innovative borders to make a pattern distinctive. Here are some of them:

The dust border: In pre-vacuum eras, rugs were often hooked of dark materials and gathered unsightly dust "mice" on the edges. Hookers solved this by creating the dust border, a wavy, light-colored edging. Nowadays, the edging can be dark or light.

Hit or miss: This variation uses strips of whatever wool has been used in the body

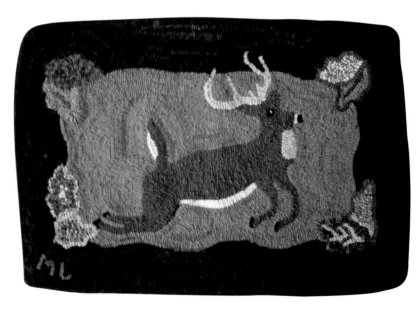

(Left) A hit-or-miss border uses strips of whatever wool was used in the body of the rug, such as in Sue Hamer's lovely original, *Color Study*. (Right) The "dust" border is illustrated on John Mather's original rug, *Deer-Mo* (first rug).

(Above) Braiding can be used as a border on a hooked rug. (Lib Callaway's *The Cow*, hooked and braided by Martha Morris.)

(Right) A wool fabric, sewn and embroidered border enhances a Kathy Morton *Chicken* pattern. Hooked by Anne Mather.

of the rug, picked up randomly and hooked. The hooking can be vertical, horizontal, or diagonal, such as in Sue Hamer's lovely original, *Color Study*.

Geometrics: Hookers were often quilters, so the patterns of one craft were borrowed by the other. Hookers thus use patchwork, clamshells (called "lamb's tongue"), and other geometrics for colorful borders.

Braided: Hookers were also often braiders, or at least familiar with the technique. Martha Morris greatly enhanced the simple Lib Callaway design *The Cow* by adding a braided border.

Wool fabric: Another nontraditional way to frame a rug is to create a mitered, wool frame. The author used this border when she didn't have enough fabric to

hook as wide a border as she wanted. It's also a great way to showcase a gorgeous fabric, and creates an alternative to simply making pillows out of small pieces. Note that some embroidered lettering—"Cluck"—was added.

Double, triple borders: Double borders are traditional: usually a single inner row of one color is used, with the rest of the frame border hooked in a second color. You can get really extravagant and add border upon border, however, such as in the enhanced version of *The Village Horse* depicted here. If you plan to do this, be sure to ask the pattern designer to give you extra fabric.

The thematic border: Jule Marie Smith, a New York fiber artist whose creations have been widely publicized, has made an art form of the themed border, one which acts almost as a visual pun of the main design of the rug. Mary Evans's border of her *Lily* rug is a good example of this border variation, as is the pine

(Above) A triple border by Martha Morris adds new life to Lib Callaway's pattern *The Village Horse*. (Left) Mary Evans's trompe l'oeil hooked rug of her dog Lily.

Mama Moose rug with pine tree border, by Anne Mather.

(Left) Rug designer Bett McLean's first rug, *Dancing Bears*, started a tradition of her trademark, twig borders. (Right) *Bee Tree*, hooked by Anne Mather, designed by Bett McLean.

tree border on *Mama Moose*. Creating themed borders is great fun and a good way for someone who has never created her own pattern to "get her feet wet."

The trademark border: Some designers—Bett McLean of Tennessee, for example

—use a variation of the same border on each rug. This only works if your designs are more or less related, as are Bett's, which feature deer, bear, and other animals.

The plaid border: You can actually hook plaids so that they remain plaids. To create this effect, you need a very large, even plaid—at least 2 inches by 2 inches—because the process of hooking will reduce the plaid 400%, making it more like a check. Cut the fabric into strips, keeping them in exactly the order you cut them. (The simplest way to do this is to cut a strip, then hook it before cutting another strip.) When you hook, notice how "far" a particular color in a plaid

hooks before it disappears, and hook the next row to match. You'll have to trust me that this is easier than it sounds, though it takes concentration. But the result is worth the effort.

Three Bears rug (above), designed by Lib Callaway, hooked by author, has a hooked plaid border. To create this effect, use a large, even plaid (left).

Wool strips can be used not only to hook your rug, but to "whip" up a border, as in *Grandchildren at the Lake*, an original by Beverly Goodrich.

Wool strips: You can also use wool strips to whip the edges of a primitive rug. This is somewhat akin to whipping the edges of a rug with tapestry wool, but uses the actual wool strips from your rug instead.

In the example above, Georgia artist Beverly Goodrich changed the colors of the border to match the interior of the rug, so that the frame actually becomes part of the picture.

Expert Tips from a Designer

- **Never be afraid to change a pattern.** "Almost all of my students in my classes change parts of patterns," says designer Patsy Becker.

- **When ordering a pattern, tell the designer to "custom-design" it for your changes.** She can, for example, leave a part blank where you know you'll be substituting something. Or the designer can leave extra background for a larger border. "Any designer who hand-draws each pattern, as I do, will be happy to do this for you," says Patsy. Be aware, however, that the border uses up a lot of background fabric (and a lot of wool), so plan accordingly and expect to pay more.

- **Make your changes first in chalk.** When you get what you want, then make the changes permanent with a black-ink marker. (Rub-A-Dub is best.) "Never use a green, red, or blue marker," Patsy says. She's found they often bleed, even when they're labeled permanent.

- **Use a damp paper towel to wipe off chalk marks.**

Don't fight your instincts:
You are most artistic when you find your "place of ease."

Lettering Tips

By Pris Buttler

Letters. We are bombarded with them. On TV, signs, newspapers, advertisements, everywhere. So why don't we see more wording on hooked rugs?

I think that we are afraid that lettering is beyond our capabilities. Not so. We are taught from kindergarten how to hand-letter. We see letters every day. They are probably one of the things with which our mind is most familiar. Our greatest limitations in hooking letters are the fabric and how much we can squeeze into a given area.

When we hook a rug, it becomes intensely personal. We all have a design we want to hook that is ours alone. Or we may find a commercial pattern we would like to add to or alter. Every rug we do has a story to tell…our story. Adding lettering about things that interest us just adds to that story.

Lettering also adds a grace and beauty that can be as attractive as the design itself. Besides complementing your design, lettering expresses ideas, emotions, and mood. To accomplish this, though, your choice of lettering needs to relate to the design and the idea being expressed. Note, for instance, that in the examples shown at right the lettering style for "antiques" looks old, and the choice for the word "child" looks childish.

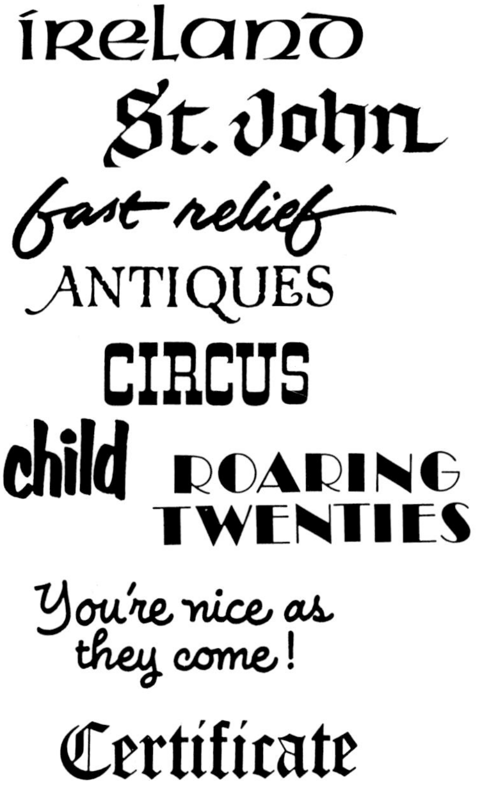
Ireland
St. John
fast relief
ANTIQUES
CIRCUS
child
ROARING TWENTIES
You're nice as they come!
Certificate

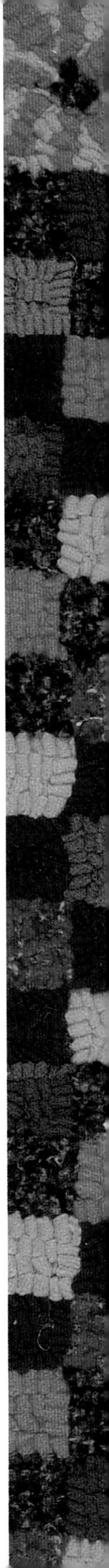

Here is my step-by-step system, from start to finish, to create lettering in your rugs. You need only practice the tips given here…and enjoy.

Parts of the Letter

At left are the correct names for some letter parts. They will be referred to several times in the instructions that follow.

Spacing

Spacing is one of the most important requirements of good lettering. It is not necessary, in creating lettering on your rug, that you exactly measure the spaces between letters. The trick is that all areas of white space between the letters of a word should *look* equal "by eye" though they need not, and actually *should not*, be absolutely equal in size.

SHADED AREA IS ONE LETTERSPACE

SHADED AREAS SHOULD LOOK EQUAL BY EYE

For example, two adjacent strokes of vertical letters are separated by the greatest measured space. In contrast, two adjacent curved letters in the same word are spaced the least measured distance apart. You can clearly see, from the

example of capital letters and their spacing shown here, that if you made all of the spaces between the letters in words equal, the result would look strange to you.

Similarly, the spaces between all small letters are not equal. To make them *look* equal, use the top and the bottom of the letter bodies, not the ascenders or descenders.

In short, "eyeballing" is really your best guide for determining spaces between letters. I have found that one to two rows of hooking between letters works best.

In addition to letter spacing, there are two other spacing considerations: word spacing and line spacing. Word spacing is the area of white space between the different words. It, too, can vary to fit words into a certain line width.

Line spacing is the space between lines, called leading (pronounced "ledding"). As hookers, we rarely place a line of text on top of another. We are most apt to use lettering in our borders.

Planning Lettering

For the timid, the number-one rule is Copy! Copy! Copy! 1) Choose text *copy* that is short—just a phrase. Nobody wants to hook long sentences. 2) Draw a line on good-quality tracing paper; then *copy* letters from magazine and newspaper ads (or the alphabets provided in this book) to the tracing paper, positioning the letters right on the line. 3) Take your lettering to your favorite *copy* shop and ask them to enlarge or reduce it to the size you specify. They will take it from there.

To get the correct size when using any alphabet, determine the height you would like your letters to be. Be sure to take into consideration that your letters expand in width as well as in height when they are enlarged. Thus, they may end up too large for the space you have allowed. If so, you may have to modify your letter spacing or choose another alphabet in which the letters are narrower (condensed). You can also solve this problem by eliminating words from the phrase. Or, if some of the words in your phrase are short (such as "and" or "the"), turn them on their sides, as I did in my rug *Our Captain Stood*.

When laying out the border that the phrase fits in, be sure to have enough pattern fabric to allow for the extra width of the lettered border. Leave enough space at the top and bottom of the phrase to hook at least 2 to 3 rows of #6-cut or the equivalent, and to bind the rug, if it is to be whip-stitched.

Work out the kinks on red-dot pattern tracing material or paper before putting it on your pattern. If you draw your letters on paper first, transfer them to red-dot, first drawing a line for your letters to sit on so they will be straight. Then trace over them with a permanent marker to transfer them to your pattern.

Alphabet Categories

Alphabets fall into one of three major categories—script, block, and gothic. Script is by far the simplest way to letter. If your handwriting is not good, perhaps you have a friend who has neat, readable script. I often letter directly onto my pattern, using a very loose version of my own handwriting.

Script
BLOCK
BLOCK Italic
GOTHIC

(Left) In *Our Captain Stood*, hooked and designed by Pris Buttler, short words are turned sideways. (Right) *Starry Night*, hooked and adapted from Van Gogh by Pris Buttler, uses a version of Pris's own handwriting in the border.

(Left) Pam Wiegand subtly incorporated her dog Molly's name into the background of her original rug, *Molly*. (Right) Decorative swashes enhance lettering, such as in Pris Buttler's border of *George Washington*.

Another very exciting way to include script is in your background, as a pattern to hook around, as Pam Wiegand did in her original rug *Molly*. Thank goodness we don't have to hook all backgrounds in straight lines or in tight little s's, c's, and squiggles. Instead, make the words "burst out" to the edge of the rug, or even lose some word beginnings and endings completely.

Block lettering constitutes most all other letters that we know—that is, those words we read daily. Gothic alphabets are rarely used these days, except for extremely formal occasions. Such alphabets are best used on certificates, Christmas items, newspaper logos, and church-related printings. Gothic letters would be the most difficult to hook and to read.

Alphabets are also distinguished by whether or not they have decorative "tails," called serifs. When letters don't have serifs, they are referred to as sans-serif letters.

ABCDEF
SERIF

ABCDEF
SANS SERIF

At the back of this book are a number of alphabets for your use, serif and sans serif. The easiest way to transfer these letters is to enlarge them first, on a copier with that capability, then trace over them for your phrase.

If you really want to have fun, copy some letters by hand. Then add some "swashes"—the wonderful, long curls on letters. I did this in *George Washington*. That rug illustrates another innovation: drawing letters so that they run over the inside border edge into the background portion of the rug.

Keep in mind that your phrases can be composed of both upper- and lower-case letters, all capital letters, or all lower case and no capitals. Mostly, have fun with lettering, but do remember to keep it as simple as possible.

Transferring Lettering to Your Rug

To transfer lettering to your rug pattern, hold your phrase up to the light. Place your first and last letter one over the other, and then fold your paper in half. Mark the middle.

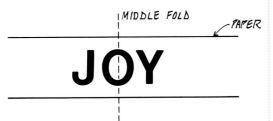

On your rug pattern, find and mark the center of the area on which you will place the words. Place the marked red-dot on the pattern. Secure it with pins or weights and trace over the lettering with a fine-point permanent marker.

It is important to remember that your fabric (monk's cloth, linen, or burlap) has a grain to it, that is, the fiber runs vertically and horizontally. If the grain does not run straight, rub your hands over the fabric to gently push the grain into place, creating as straight a line as possible. Drawing directly onto the cloth grain with a marker gives your letters a line on which to sit. When tracing vertical letters, place them on the vertical grain as well. It is very important to follow the grain—even if it doesn't look straight to the eye. When you hook on the grain, especially with linen or burlap, the finished rug will be straight.

If your phrase is to go on all four sides of the pattern, make the middle centering marks on each side, following the steps above.

When running phrases on all sides of the pattern, face the letters toward the center of the work, including the bottom line. It is harder to read on display but more pleasing to the eye, and the border then becomes a frame for the picture inside. If the phrases are only to go at the top and/or bottom, place them "right reading," that is, bottoms of the letters toward the bottom of the pattern.

Do not stack lettering café style, that is, one letter above the other. You might be tempted to do this on the sides of the pattern when space is tight, but it is very hard to read.

When putting phrases on all sides of a border, face the letters—even those on the bottom line—toward the center portion of the pattern. It is harder to read, but more pleasing to the eye. Rug: *Our Captain Stood,* hooked and designed by Pris Buttler.

A detail from *Sampler of Faith*, hooked by Pam Wiegand, designed by Pris Buttler, illustrates Buttler's technique for hooking letters around a curve.

Laying Letters on a Curve

Laying out lettering on a curve is simple. Remember your mark at the center of your phrase? You will use it again, placing center-mark to center-mark. On a rectangular pattern, as your letters move around the curve, slit your red-dot or paper between each letter, but do not cut the letter completely loose. (This is similar to sewing, when you snip seams to create ease.)

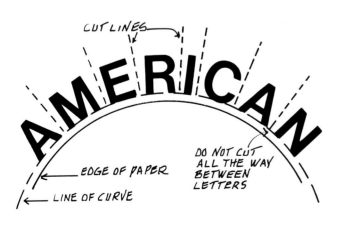

Leave a little red-dot attached at the top of the letters (or bottom, depending upon which way your letters face). Gently bend the letter around, easing it into place. You may have to do this between each letter on the curve. On an oval or circular pattern, all spacing between letters may need to be split.

Hooking Letters

Allow space for at least 2–3 rows of hooking at the top and bottom of letters; otherwise, your lettering will look crowded. In other words, when transferring the letters to your pattern, leave the equivalent of 2–3 rows of #6-cut and then draw a line on which to rest your letters. (You can hook these rows before your lettering, if you wish.)

Letter-space allowance: leave room for 1–2 rows of hooked background around each letter. Letters look best if

Lessons on Lettering—Some Highlights

- Eyeballing is your best guide for determining spaces between letters.

- Keep any lettering short. Nobody wants to hook long sentences.

- Following the grain is very important—even if it doesn't look straight to the eye.

- Letters look best if you hook two rows within the body of the letter.

- Consider using two colors for each letter and a smaller cut for the outline color.

- Allow space for at least two to three rows of hooking at the top and bottom of letters. Some people prefer to hook these rows before doing the letters.

- Allow one to two rows of hooking between letters.

- Hook two or three letters—and the background around them—each time you sit down to work.

- If your letters look lost after you have hooked-in the background around them, take them out and re-hook them. This will really make them stand out.

you hook two rows within the body of the letter. Note the alphabets later in the book. The letters are thicker on one side than on the other; the diagonal may also be thicker or thinner, depending upon the alphabet. After you have hooked letters and the background around them, the letters may be "crisper" if you take them out and re-hook them.

Using a narrow cut of wool, outline each letter in a complementary color, either lighter or darker than the background color. Then, using a wider cut, fill in the letter with the same color or another color. Hook a light-colored letter against a dark background or a dark letter against a light background. Or, a warm color (yellows, oranges, orange-reds, yellow-greens, yellow-browns, turquoise blues) next to a cool color (purples, rosy reds, purple-blues, grays, gray-browns). Such color combinations will really make your lettering "pop."

If your lettering has curves, hook *directionally* when outlining and filling. This applies to swashes or any other curves within letters, such as C, D, G, J, O, Q, S, and U.

I tend to hook two or three letters in a work each time I sit down to hook. This way, the lettering doesn't become such an awesome task at the end of the rug. As you hook the letters, also fill in the background around them.

"You're not trying to be realistic—you're playing with color.
If you want a realistic picture, get a camera."
—SUE HAMER

Playing with Color and Texture: Four Artists, Four Unique Styles

Color and texture are the very essence of the rug-hooking experience. Or, as designer Charlotte Price put it, "Color is the joy of hooking."

How a fiber artist chooses and handles her colored woolens—how she "plays" with color and texture—can be very idiosyncratic. It can become her signature, so to speak. Think of Joan Moshimer…Jule Marie Smith…Patricia Merikallio…Patty Yoder…Roslyn Logsdon…Polly Minick…all of them have very distinctive, in some cases clearly recognizable, styles.

So what exactly do rug hookers *do* to create such differences? Ultimately, of course, we can't answer this. As Howard Norman wrote, about art, in his award-winning novel *The Bird Artist*, "The mystery of it's way bigger than the science of it." But that won't stop us from trying. So, in this section, we'll showcase four artists who hook very different subjects in very different ways and see if we can isolate some elements of their styles.

Missey and Molly, hooked and designed by Sue Hamer. (Pattern available from Charco Patterns.)

Sue Hamer: Mixing Precision with Creative Clutter

Sue Hamer teaches and practices rug hooking in St. Charles, Illinois, a scenic town in the Fox River Valley, about an hour from Chicago. She has hooked for 25 years.

When Sue, a self-admitted scrounger, started hooking, she used only old cloth. "I was born in the Depression," she says, "and my mother's middle name was frugal. I never threw anything away." The epitome of this "You've got it, so use it" mentality is her charming rug of her two cats, Missey and Molly. Though her pets

Color Study and close-up, hooked and designed by Sue Hamer, illustrates her sophisticated color palate, created with a variety of cuts and colors.

(Below) Sue Hamer starts with graph paper, felt-tip colored pens, and lots of leftovers to create one of her studies in color. (Right) Close-up from a Sue Hamer original, *Mockbird*.

were actually calicos, Sue hooked them in black-and-whites, tweeds and grays because "that's the wool [she] had."

Nowadays, Sue does not have the time to hunt for old clothes, but she still has bags of leftovers. These she supplements with new wool purchases, especially Dorr's new light plaids and checks, which she overdyes. The bags of leftovers consist of a variety of colors and cuts (3's through 6's). Sue's approach is to use them to create sophisticated color palates, especially geometric designs.

What fascinates me about Sue is the contrast between the precision of her

rug designs and the creative clutter involved in making them! She designs most of her patterns, or "color studies," by creating quilts of color on graph paper with felt-tip colored pens. Then she has to transfer the patterns to the background fabric, such as burlap or linen. She then scrounges through her leftovers, combining many shades of each color. (This is not unlike Kaffe Fassett's technique for knitting; like that artist, Sue may have ten greens creating a green square.) When she turns this technique from geometrics and color studies to more traditional subjects—as in her *Mockbird*, for example, or *Six Hearts*—you can see the glorious richness that this mix of color produces.

Six Hearts, hooked and designed by Sue Hamer, shows how a mix of color adds richness to a simple pattern.

Linda Mather: Bold Color, Simple Design

A style that is simple but flamboyant: it sounds like an oxymoron. But both words describe the style of Linda Mather, a new hooker (less than 2 years) from Sautee-Nacoochee Valley, Georgia.

Linda works and has a family, not to mention seven very consuming interests:

two horses, three golden Labs, and two cats. Whether this influences her style, I don't know, but all of her patterns—usually originals, drawn for her by her husband John, an artist—are arrestingly simple in design. The borders are usually plain frames or thematic. Linda relies mostly on thrift shop pants and skirts, supplementing these, when necessary, with dyed wool from her teacher,

Horse with Brands, hooked and designed by Linda Mather.

(Above) *Flying Cowgirl*, hooked by Linda Mather; designed by her son, Nathanial.
(Below) *Old Betsy*, hooked and designed by Linda Mather.

Bronc in Sunset, hooked by Linda Mather, adapted from an antique matchbox cover.

Mary Williamson. For *Old Betsy*, Linda achieved the found-in-the-attic white effect by dyeing white skirts in tea bags. The red strips were achieved by marrying. The latter is a process of steeping wools and linings together in a pot, with a teaspoon of detergent without bleach, to make them bleed into one another. The result is a mixture of wools that work well together but are not all the exact same color. Other examples of Linda's married wool are the background in *Horse with Brands* (page 68) and the sun, sky, and waves in *Bronc in Sunset* (*above*).

Lately Linda has started to do traditional dyeing, using Cushing dyes. She loves it and usually has three pots of colors going at once. Happily, her dyeing keeps the vibrancy and starkness apparent in her earlier rugs.

Finally, Linda hooks using a wide cut (size 6 or, preferably, 8 strip) and very pronounced lines to fill in her backgrounds. The result is a sort of primitive elegance (another oxymoron?). Her style is the essence of the primitive look that is so desirable right now—yet it is very distinctive. And Linda's style of hooking —designing her own patterns, using thrift-shop wools, marrying wools, hooking with wide-cut—is a valuable reminder that, as with the pioneer women who perfected this craft, less is often more.

"Color is a very personal thing—it is a sensation to be felt."

—STELLA HAY REX

Martha Morris:
Simple Dyeing Palette,
Hand-Cutting

This veteran hooker's penchant for adapting patterns has already been discussed at length. But Martha has some more tricks up her sleeve, ones that contribute to a very distinctive, brilliantly colored style.

At right is a close-up of Martha's version of *Stella Hay Rex*, a rug shown in its entirety on page 16 of the opening gallery. For this rug, only three dye colors were used: Cushing's union (not today's acid) colors of Old Gold, Bronze-Green, and Egyptian Red. Indeed, virtually all of Martha's seventy-plus rugs were dyed in wools steeped in only these three dyes. The rest of her colors are as-is, such as the tweed used in the tree trunk in *Sassafras Tree*, on the next page.

So how does she achieve her vibrant potpourri of color? By using these dyes "over every color in the rainbow." Martha almost never uses off-the-bolt; she feels it lacks character. What she does use is as-is: she has a thirty-year accumulation of tweeds, checks, plaids, and solids stored in her basement. She overdyes these in batches of various textures and colors, a technique she learned in Alice Beatty's kitchen. (Beatty co-authored a bible of hooking, *Basic Rug Hooking*,

Close-up of *Stella Hay Rex*, a Lib Callaway pattern, hooked by Martha Morris. Only three dye colors were used in this rug.

which was first published in 1977 under the title *The Hook Book*; it is still in print.) Martha also learned from Beatty to throw a strip of white in at the tail end of a dyeing project; it will pick up just enough color to blend in, something stark white never does.

"Many shades of a few colors tend to make a rug restful," Martha explains,

Sassafras Tree, hooked by Martha Morris, designed by Lib Callaway.

quoting designer Stella Hay Rex. "Too many hues tend to make the rug advance rather than keep its place on the floor."

One result of this dyeing technique is that all her colors work well together—not just within a rug, but from rug to rug. As an example, she did not dye any wool

for her version of Patsy Becker's *Sailing Away:* she used leftovers from other projects to create the stunning rainbow array of clouds and other features that make this one of her favorite rugs.

Another factor that contributes to the unique appearance of Martha's rugs

is that she hand-cuts all of her wools. The only exception would be when she needs a size-3 cut for a detail. Here she quotes Stella Rex, the rug's namesake—and in Martha's opinion one of the greatest rug designers:

> *You need some of the irregularity that comes only from hand-cutting. That slight lack of perfect coordination between the hand and the eyes, resulting in uneven strips, contributes to texture in the rug. To be told of a handcrafted product, "It looks as perfect as if it had been made by machine," is scarcely complimentary.*

I think that this is a valuable piece of advice, and one that perfectionists need to hear: Rug hookers are *not* after perfection. They're after art. And the two are definitely not synonymous.

In her years of studying with and under some of the masters of rug hooking, Martha has absorbed a wealth of knowledge. Here are a few insights from the experts:

- **A varied texture is pleasing, but if overdone it can be tiring.**

- **Be sure to include neutrals in a rug; they make it rich.**

- **Use pure colors only in touches.**

- **Repetition of color is a simple way to strengthen good design.**

- **Always plan what colors you will use, and where, in a rug; but *never* "color plan" at night.**

Martha Morris used leftovers from other projects to create this stunning rug, *Sailing Away*, designed by Patsy Becker.

"A good portrait...has more than just accurate features.
It has some other thing."

—ALICE NEEL

Rebecca Knudsen: Trusting Her Instincts

Our fourth featured artist is Rebecca Knudsen, a rug hooker from Provo, Utah. Rebecca taught herself to rug hook. Her first rug was 5 by 6 feet. ("I didn't know any better," she says.) It sold. Rebecca is now a self-supporting rug hooker, doing mostly commissioned work.

Three of her rugs have appeared in *Rug Hooking* magazine's national "Celebrations" contest (Celebrations III, IV, and V). And I saved the best for last: She has six children.

Rebecca Knudsen's prayer rug *Jacob*.

I'm featuring Rebecca in this section (you will meet her again in the section on hooking children) because she has adapted the admittedly lengthy process of rug hooking into a very busy life by concentrating only on those aspects she most enjoys: design, color, and expressing herself. Earlier, I spoke of "finding your place of ease"—trusting your instincts—with rug hooking. Rebecca Knudsen has done this—with spectacular results.

Let me give some examples. Rebecca does not hand-cut; she uses a machine and then only an 8-cut because she does not like having to change the blade. Nor does she dye; in fact, she avoids it at all costs. Her busy lifestyle also doesn't allow time for thrift-shop "foraging." She buys all her wool. So she must have a roomful, all organized, right? No. "I have wool under my bed, behind the TV, in drawers. [But] My kids are still home; when they start moving out, I've got *great* plans," she says, laughing.

"If I thought I had to dye, I'd be in real trouble," Rebecca admits. "I love the design part, so that's where I choose to spend my time and trouble. Rug hooking is just a vehicle to express whatever you want it to express. It's not the most important part. What you're expressing is."

Rebecca believes strongly in trusting your instincts. "You have to be really careful that you don't stop trusting your ability to create. I've seen that time and time again, especially with women. We don't trust what's inside of us, our ability to express very personal things."

In addition to design, Rebecca loves the vibrancy of rug hooking. "Colors are so important," she says—something to which her rugs attest. In her prayer rug portraits of her children, for example, each color palette was picked with the child's personality in mind. (Three are shown here; three in the section on hooking children.)

To obtain the colors she wants, Rebecca buys a lot of wool. "Whenever I see wool on sale, I buy. I've learned not to say, 'I'll never use that.' If I like it, I buy it," she says. She also buys from wool suppliers who advertise in *Rug Hooking* magazine. (Suppliers will send sample swatches of their inventory upon request.) And if she needs something specific, she doesn't hesitate to get it, because "in the long run, what's a few more dollars?"

And although Rebecca does not dye, she does *remove* color, by using detergent (identical to the process of marrying, described in the section on Linda Mather; remove the fabric when it has faded to the color you want. Note: Pris Buttler, another designer, uses baking soda to remove color). For example, in Rebecca's prayer rug of her daughter Ashley, this artist knew she wanted a specific rusty-red fabric she had seen as the background, but she wanted lighter tones as well. "Removing color really helped me get the shades and varieties I wanted in that rug," she said.

Another feature that is distinctive of Rebecca's style is lettering—usually inspirational, either from the Bible or Mormon scripture. "I've always loved words, always used them," she says. In fact, her educational background and degree are in designing typography and print. She uses all styles of lettering—upper and lower

Rebecca
Knudsen's prayer
rug *Katy*.

Rebecca
Knudsen's prayer
rug *Ashley*.

Rug Hooking: Too Expensive?

I've only heard two complaints about rug hooking. One is that it's messy.

My teacher Mary Williamson's response to that, when a student raised the point in a class, was "Listen here, I'm here to turn you on. We'll worry about vacuuming later." Enough said.

The second concern—cost—is a valid one for many, especially beginning hookers. So here are some ways to make this art more affordable and thus accessible:

- Hand-cut your wool.

- Shop in thrift shops—especially on sale days.

- Tell everyone you know you're a rug hooker. When people clean out their closets, they'll think of you. (And you can reward them, in return, with a hooked ornament, mat, or pin.)

- Start marrying wools to add and subtract color. You do this by putting the colors you want to affect in a steaming pot of water with 1 teaspoon of detergent without bleach. Add vinegar when you're happy with the colors, and cook for another 20 minutes.

- Learn to dye. More than 50% of the price of dyed woolens is the cost of dye and labor to the teacher who dyed it—and she earned every penny of it.

- Have swap days with other hookers where you trade a color you have too much of for one you need.

- Hook on monk's cloth instead of linen: it's significantly cheaper. Cheapest of all is burlap.

- Design some of your own patterns.

case, cursive, print—and likes to introduce a variety of color tones into the letters "to add a little more interest."

Rebecca likes the forgivingness of rug hooking, the fact that the medium of wool—perhaps because it can't be controlled the way a paintbrush can—has a compensating charm. Indeed, her "mistakes" often turn into favorite parts of a rug, as with the exaggerated fingers and hands of her daughters Katy and Ashley. She worried about these aspects of their portraits "more than the faces" while she was creating them. Only afterwards did she realize how much she liked these larger-than-life hands. Subconsciously, she believes, she had emphasized what is very important to each girl: Katy is a harpist; Ashley, an artist.

That experience taught this artist to be careful not to pull out too much. "Let it [what you think is a mistake] go. ...Maybe it will grow into something that you will really like," she advises.

"We want everything to be perfect, but children aren't. That's what excited me about these [prayer] rugs. They're not perfect," she says.

Learning to Let Go

Unlike needlepoint or cross-stitch, the goal of rug hooking is not perfection. Most new hookers, especially ones who have come from other fiber or needle arts, need to loosen up. Here are some tips for doing that:

◆ Hand-cut all or a part of your project.

◆ If you find yourself in a perfectionist, rip-out mode, put the rug on the wall or floor and back up several feet. This is how the rug will actually be seen when it is finished. Does it look a lot better than it did up close? Try to remember this when you're hooking. (You can also buy a tool called a reducer, the opposite of a magnifying glass, which gives you the at-a-distance perspective.)

◆ When you think that something you've hooked—a face, in particular—looks funny or awful, leave it anyway. Continue to hook around it. Often your "mistakes" look wonderful once the surrounding area is filled in.

◆ Cut a number of different wools in related colors or values—say, grays and browns for a tree trunk, various shades of green for grass. Now close your eyes and randomly pick up strips and hook. You will be amazed how real and lifelike objects appear when hooked this way, and it's a lot easier on you. Remind yourself that uneven stitches and less-than-perfect designs add to a piece's charm.

◆ Create a sampler of as-is material. It will be a catalyst to your being freer in the use of a variety of textures.

Rug hooking teacher Sharon Townsend's sampler of as-is materials helps students see the effects that different fabrics create when hooked. Idea for sampler: Joan Moshimer.

Creating Your
Own Patterns

Sandy Myers used her award-winning mini-quilt, *Bethany Gardens* (above),
to create her first rug of the same name (below).

Hooking What You Love

So far we have discussed technique, color, texture, and certain design elements involved in the creative process of rug hooking. But there is one element of design we have largely ignored, though it may be the most important: subject. For we hook what we love.

We have all met her—or been there. The fiber artist who can't stop hooking horses …or houses…or cats…or…well, you fill in the blank. Certain subjects just call to us again and again—our own sirens, if you will.

"Obsessions are interesting," says that marvelously quixotic and wise character Zoe in Joanna Trollope's novel *Next of Kin*. "And we all need them," as my friend Carol Walters says. I know of no hooker who would argue with her. For me, bears and deer have been the catalysts for more rugs than I will admit to. This has nothing, obviously, to do with decorating one's house; no one *needs* another bear rug. Our hands simply itch to create certain things. And when we hook what we love, we love what we hook.

Choosing a subject that you love is a natural first step in creating your own patterns. Thus, when veteran Georgia quilter Sandy Myers decided to take up rug hooking, her first project was—what else?—a rug of a quilt. She chose six of the motifs from her award-winning mini-quilt, *Bethany Gardens*, to form her pattern for her first rug.

If you are not good at sketching or design, there are several avenues you can take. Probably the most common is to work from a photo of a favorite subject —such as a pet or home. Children's artwork is also the inspiration for many hooked pieces. Uncopyrighted artwork, especially that found in clip-art books, is an invaluable resource. Pamphlets of clip art range in subject matter from animals to holiday themes and everything in between; they are available from any large bookstore for a modest price. And don't overlook children's coloring books as a wonderful source of templates— that is, ready-to-trace common objects for your rugs, such as trees, wagons, or animals.

Or, you can do all of the above, and then some. This is what hooker Marilyn

A grandchild's piece of artwork inspired Pat Tritt's hooked pillow (above).

Bottjer did to create her rug *Carpe Diem*. Its inspiration came from an ancient sundial on the side of a building in Alsace, France, that had "carpe diem" carved on the ribbon above it. Marilyn took a photo of this site. One of her students, who was studying computer graphics, scanned it into the computer, along with images of the sun and moon. The stars and the shooting star were clip art. From several printed-out versions, Marilyn chose her favorite. The student then printed the pattern out, in pieces, onto a number of 8½-by-11-inch sheets, which Marilyn taped together to create her full-size pattern.

Several subjects are such common themes among hookers that they seem integral to the art. Such is the case with children, animals (pets in particular), and houses. So let's look at how different fiber artists have approached these subjects and see what techniques of theirs might work for us and our vision.

The pattern for *Carpe Diem*, an original by Marilyn Bottjer, was inspired by an ancient site in France and finely tuned on a computer.

Children in Wide-Cut Wool

Certainly children are among the most popular subjects of all art, and rug hooking is no exception. But hooking children presents unique challenges. Children's bodies and heads have different proportions than those of adults, for example. And attempts to make hooked children look exactly like specific children may seem next to impossible. Our "brush," after all, is often a ¼-inch-wide strip of wool.

But rug hooking's inherent lack of precision is part of its charm—as well as an impetus to be more creative, to compensate. And so, rugs depicting children are among the most endearing. In this section, we will show you some examples of hooking children with wide-cut wool (6 or higher) and lead you through the creation of an original paper-doll rug.

Because it can be very difficult to make a hooked face actually look like a specific child, the hooker's task is to capture the essence of the child rather than the child itself. Notice, for example, how

Hooked rugs *Remember Me* (left) and *Little Bo Peep* (next page, top) convey qualities about children even without showing facial features.

The color choices in Rebecca Knudsen's prayer rug *Ann* (below) convey the child's personality.

this was accomplished in the two rugs *Remember Me* and *Little Bo Peep*. Each of these rugs strongly conveys emotions about the children—despite the fact that the children's faces lack features.

One way this is accomplished is through the color palette used in a rug. *Remember Me*'s serge blues and parchment background are subdued, but warm, secure. *Little Bo Peep*'s vibrant pinks, purples, and yellows, on the other hand, mimic the frolicking design and manage to radiate happiness and youth.

Similarly, in Rebecca Knudsen's prayer rug *Ann*, the deep purples, reds, and yellow-golds all convey the exuberance of the central figure. "Ann's very verbal, so emotional," Rebecca offers. "I wanted to express that not only through the picture but the color."

The color and choice of a child's clothes also communicate personality and character. In Sandy Gannett's rug *Joey*, for example, the rug hooker's grandson just had to be featured in denim. Sandy felt this so strongly that she actually hooked the jeans in medium-weight

Clothes convey personality, as in *Joey*, a rug hooked and designed by Sandy Gannett.

denim. "It was really hard to hook with," she concedes. "It had no give. But it had a wonderful effect."

In my own daughter Jean's angel rug, I also hooked her in jeans—as well as a pink angora sweater and running shoes. These say a lot more about her than a flowing gown would. Similarly, young Ann's red-striped sweater in Knudsen's rug *Ann* has a T-shirt feel. And Knudsen deliberately introduced a lot of movement into Jordan's handknit-looking

The environment surrounding a hooked child conveys personality, as in *Jean Angel*, the author's adaptation of Marion Ham's *The Littlest Angel*.

(Left) *Jordan* and (right) *Benjamin*, prayer rugs hooked and designed by Rebecca Knudsen.

sweater—together with a lot of curving lines in the entire rug—to portray that daughter's "very emotional" side.

A third way to communicate a child's personality is his or her environment. What things does she love? What toys does he play with? What dreams does this child have? Jean in *Jean Angel*, for example, is flying over the city lights: if you had any doubts, you now know for sure that she is our "party girl." Joey has his wagon; Gannett's other grandson, Nikolas, has his blocks, balloon, and bear. The environments of Knudsen's rugs are especially rich with symbols of each child, many spiritual in nature.

Nikolas, hooked and designed by Sandy Gannett.

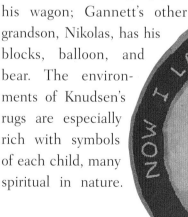

In *Benjamin*, for example, the quotation and symbols are taken from 1 Kings 17. This artist, in fact, used an inspirational quotation from either the Bible or Mormon scripture in each of her prayer rugs. Each quotation symbolizes a child, but also, as it winds its way around the rug, seems to protect—be a prayer for—the child.

What the rugs we've looked at thus far illustrate is that hooking can convey a child's personality and character before you've even drawn a face or body. Color, clothes, and the symbols and environment in which you set the child all serve to achieve this.

By using color, clothes, and symbols, a rug hooker can convey personality and character without even showing facial features.

Hooking faces: I have always felt that children look as cute from behind as they do from the front. If you doubt me, look at the child—with her outstretched, mittened hand—in *Christmas Is a Coming*. Nevertheless, even I have to admit that there comes a time when a hooker must learn to hook a face. So let's take this task head-on (so to speak).

Keep a photo of your child handy as a visual aid. Hook the outline of the hair first; this acts as a holding line so the face doesn't "grow."

Then assemble your flesh tones. Dorr Mills (a source of moth-proofed hooking wool for decades) sells a reasonably priced set of hand-dyed, pinkish-flesh wools that are nicely mottled (thus

Christmas Is a Coming, hooked by Anne Mather; designed by Jane Flynn (Charco patterns).

(Left) Samples of Cushing wools available for black and brown skin-toned hooked figures.
(Right) This close-up from Sandy Gannett's original rug, *Gabriella*, illustrates the simplest hooked eye: closed.

producing a natural looking shading). If you're dyeing yourself, recommended swatches (a 6- or 8-value package of dyed wool) for Caucasian flesh tones are Cox 63 and 36, available from Jane Olsen. In addition, Emma Lou Lais and Barbara Carroll have two flesh formulas (flesh and peachy flesh) in their dye book, *Antique Colours for Primitive Rugs*.

For darker skin tones, Cushing sells a #7 dark and medium brown spot-dye. This hookers' resource also sells a changing variety of tweeds, which work well for brown and black skin tones. Finally, rug-hooking teachers are familiar with unpublished formulas—such as those developed by Ethyl Bruce and others— to dye the flesh colors you need for a rug.

Use a darker hue to outline the face, and a lighter tone for the face itself. For black skin, find a brown or tan that matches the skin tone; a subtle purple or a darker brown fabric works well for outlining and highlights. Even if you hook in an 8-cut, drop to a smaller cut for the face; the smaller cut should be used to outline.

Now hook the eyes. The simplest method, which Gannett used in her two grandchildren's rugs, *Nikolas* and *Gabriella*, is to hook a simple, upside-down curve, as if the child's eyes are closed. The sideways eye is also easy. If you are doing open eyes, Betty Laine's technique is simple and adapts well to most faces (see boxed sidebar opposite).

Don't be alarmed if the eyes look bulbous and bug-eyed. You cannot judge the face until all the features and skin are hooked. Most faces look horrible at first. Just trust the system.

Now hook the nose—the less the better. A suggestion of a curve or line with the darker skin hue—such as was used to outline the face—is fine. Don't hook nostrils; they simply end up looking piggish. Last, hook the mouth. Veteran South Carolina teacher Margaret Howell recommends you use just a few stitches in a hue one shade darker than the skin; usually anything more

Three Simple Eyes

Closed: **This consists of a simple "smiley" curve. This is the simplest eye.**

Sideways: **If your child is being shown from the side, one sideways eye works well. Hook the L-portion in a tone that blends with the skin but is darker. Use color or a dot of black for the spherical part. Hook with flesh color up to the spherical part.**

Open: **This is Betty Laine's method of creating an open eye. Using gray or tan (never black) and using a 3- to 5-cut, depending on the size of the face:**

a.   **Create a curved top lash (skip the bottom lid: it looks like eyeliner). Put a small, defining mark at each outside corner.**

b.   **Hang the iris (round part of eye) from the center of the lid; *never* show the complete circle. (That's what makes a face look angry or crazed.)**

c.   **Hook one row of eye color around the outside of the pupil. Then hook the pupil black, with a highlight in white (a piece of thread, knotted, will do). By hooking the pupil last, you keep it from getting too large.**

d.   **Put a few stitches on either side of the iris to represent the whites of the eyes.**

e.   **Add eyebrows.**

Betty Laine's technique for finely hooking eyes and face. Pattern: *Little Sister*, by Jane Flynn (Charco Patterns); hooking by Mary Williamson.

than two shades darker is too stark and makes the child look like a Kewpie Doll.

Now begin filling in around each of the features to rein them in, make them more defined. Hook directionally, that is, concentrically, from inside to outside, never in straight lines. You may want to work a light pink or rose in for cheekbones. When you have finished the face, if it still looks weird, then correct.

This is basically how you hook a face in wide-cut. If you plan to use fine-cut (2- to 4-cut) and shading, diagrams exist in other books or sources that will lead you through the process.

A Hooked Child:
The Paper Doll Rug

Like many creations, the *Paper Doll Rug* was born of necessity and frustration. I was once a quilter, and saved both of my daughters' dresses and outfits to some-day make *Sunbonnet Sue* quilts for them. Then two things happened. One, I quit quilting and started hooking. Second, some of the cutest clothes were lost; others, when I dug them out of the closet, were so precious I could not bear to cut them up. So, by hooking rugs featuring my daughters as paper dolls, I figured I would get a keepsake of the children in their favorite outfits, but still get to keep the clothes for posterity.

But I was intimidated. An out-of-proportion flower is one thing, but a child? Gail Loder—head of the art

Autumn paper doll rug, hooked and designed by Gail Loder.

department at Rabun Gap-Nacoochee School (the originator of the *Foxfire* books)—understands this all too well. Her daughter Brooke, when she first glimpsed Gail's first attempt at capturing her in wool, responded, "You're doing this to get back at me for the teenage years, right?"

As with the earlier rugs of children we've studied, however, the paper doll rug works in part by illusion: if you get the right color for the hair and eyes; get the face structure (i.e., round, oval, square) accurate; and suggest the basic body type (slim, stocky; short, tall), you're halfway there. Your child's participation—choosing favorite outfits, for example—will complete the picture and make your son or daughter feel it "looks just like me."

Well, it isn't *quite* that easy. My first

attempts were a new phenomenon in hooking: the primitive alien. Then Gail shared some artistic tips. She taught me basic proportions of the human body and face (see box page 95). I never knew, for example, that five heads is the height of the average young child's body…or that five eyes could fit across the face at the point where our eyes our set. It is amazing what a difference getting these proportions down right makes in the verisimilitude of a finished child or paper doll. A note on these statistics, however: These are an *aid*. If your paper doll child's eyes look like they are floating in her forehead, looking at the chart will explain why. If the child looks top-heavy, noting that children's body proportions differ from adults is helpful. But please don't feel you have to adhere to rigid rules: this is simply to elucidate, not for you to imitate!

Gail has also designed templates for popular outfits—ranging from dresses and jeans to ballet outfits, PJ's, and raincoats. (See Projects and Patterns section.) Each can be personalized to your child. Enlarge them on a copier machine to get a rug the size of the *Brooke* and *Autumn* rugs, that is, 22 by 34 inches.

To create a paper doll rug of your child, start by looking through photo albums of your child, helping her (or him) choose favorite outfits. Pull the photos of about ten; then try arranging them around the doll figure to find the layout that works best. You will probably have to weed them down to four to six outfits—one for the body, the others to surround it. This will create a rug approximately the size of ours. If you want to feature more outfits, either enlarge the rug or make the paper doll and clothes smaller.

Brooke paper doll rug, hooked and designed by Gail Loder.

Exaggerate
clothing details,
as in these
close-ups from
Anne Mather's
paper doll rugs
for her daughters
Maggie and
Jeannie.

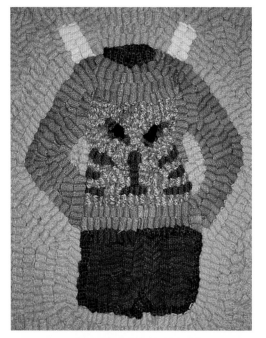

When you have chosen the outfits that you think will look best, alter the templates to match your child's clothes. Keep this process simple. Exaggerate details you know the child loved—as I did, for example, with the scowling cat on my daughter Maggie's favorite hand-knit sweater and the ducks on Jeannie's smocked dress. Don't feel the compulsion to make every sleeve the right length, or the colors exact. Do add tabs:

they help create the illusion of a paper doll. Once you have altered your clothes, arrange and rearrange until you have a pleasing layout, using as guides our four rugs, if you wish, or the patterns in the back section.

On a large sheet of paper, mark off the perimeter of your rug, drawing a 2- to 2.5-inch border inside it. Now glue (I use removable glue on a stick) your templates and doll in the layout you have chosen. Do consider colors in your lay-out—you don't want all your blues in one area, all your reds in another. And be sure to leave some space between outfits so that the rug isn't crowded-looking.

Now, work in the child's name. The amount of outfits you have chosen will dictate whether the name goes within the rug or on the border and whether you use the first name only or add the last name. You can use any style of lettering (see lettering samples at back of book), including a childlike scrawl.

In the border, sign your initials or "Mom" in your handwriting, and the date. Both Gail and I tried numerous borders in perfecting the paper doll style. Rejected were hit-or-miss borders and ones incorporating favorite toys: both were too busy. Ultimately, we both settled on simple borders; they didn't detract from the doll and her clothes.

When you're happy with your final draft, transfer it to red-dot. (This Pellon-weight pattern-tracing fabric is widely available at fabric stores. Place it over your draft and trace with a black perma-nent marker.) Then secure (with pins or tape) the red-dot pattern onto your back-ground material—burlap, linen, rug warp, or cotton monk's cloth—and trace again. After removing the red-dot, you may need to redraw some lines to make them show up enough on your actual pattern.

Hook the Doll First

Start with the doll. There are two reasons for this. One, it's in the center of the rug, and you should always begin in the center so that your rug lies flat. But just as important, the child is the most difficult part of the piece. When you have captured her, you'll love working on her clothes, which work up more easily.

Hook the face, as discussed above. Then do the hair. Try to get the color right and use highlights. Try also to capture your child's hairstyle. A child's hair is one of her most defining features, so give it the attention it deserves.

Then outline the entire body in the darkest flesh hue or, if necessary, a thin row of brown. (Gail prefers outlining the whole doll in black.) Drop a little curve on each knee in the dark hue, also. Then fill in. You may use a larger cut—a 5 or 6. You have to experiment. Don't pack, or your child's legs will become quite stout!

Hooking the Clothes

When hooking the clothes, keep your photos handy. You do not need to have an exact shade of a dress or outfit, just one

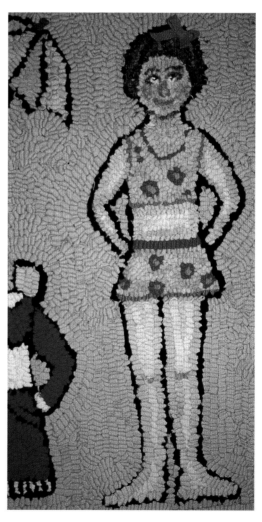

Outlining the doll makes it stand out.

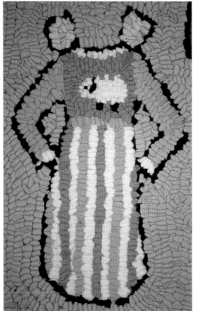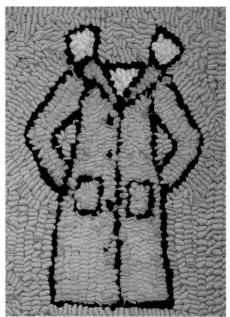

Outlining each outfit adds a crisp-ness to the design.

that's close. Do use a denim blue for jeans, though. Note that a large plaid will hook as a check. For example, the green dress that Jeannie wears in her paper doll rug was actually a gingham check, but this would be complicated to do in a small area. By using a large green-and-white plaid, I suggested the check. Overemphasize details such as stripes, lace, scalloped edges, and appliqués, but simplify them. Outlining each outfit adds a crispness to the design and makes it look more like a cut-out Add any props (pendants, balls, etc.), then hook tabs in an off-white or cream color.

Backgrounds and Borders

Background colors and borders will be dictated by the colors of the clothes you include. I usually choose background and border colors before beginning a rug; the paper doll rug was an exception. Both Gail and I found that so many colors and details went into these designs

that the choices of background and border colors were best made after the details were hooked. As a general rule, a neutral (e.g., parchment, light green-blue, or yellow) seems to work best for the background. Gail varied the back-ground in her *Brooke* rug (page 91), suggesting wallpaper—a darling detail. But she was not able to incorporate this feature into her other daughter's rug (page 90), where it would have been too busy and difficult to work around objects.

Of all the rugs I have hooked, the paper doll ones are my favorites. They provide such a treasure trove of memo-ries—perhaps one reason our girls (now in college) love them too. I will never part with them—except to the girls themselves one day—so I've devised a way to share them. I had photos of them color-copied onto card stock paper. Sets of these cards make wonderful gifts for grandparents, and I enjoy sending indi-vidual cards to friends.

How to Draw a Child's Face

AUTHOR'S NOTE: *Gail Loder, head of the art department at Rabun-Gap Nacoochee School, devised an explanation of proportions and placement of features on a young child's face. This drawing and the accompanying explanations are meant to help you isolate problems in your drawing and serve as guides, not to imitate.* **Precision is <u>not</u> the goal of primitive hooking.**

1. Draw a standing egg-shaped oval or rounded oval.

2. Divide this oval in half, horizontally, with a light line (Line A).

3. Divide the oval in half vertically (Line B).

4. Center the eyes on Line A. If you put the eyes higher than this they will appear to be "floating" in the forehead—which is a common error.

5. A secret for eyes is the spacing: five eyes could exactly fit across Line A. You usually place the two eyes at positions 2 and 4 on that line.

6. Divide the top half of the oval in half horizontally (Line C); where lines C and B intersect is the hairline.

7. Add an arch above each eye for eyebrows. These extend from the inside corner of the eyes to slightly past the outside edge of the eyes.

8. Divide the bottom half of the oval in half horizontally (Line D).

9. Drop a light or invisible line down from each of the inside corners of the eyes to meet Line D. This is where you put the nose. The nostrils lie on Line D (if you put them—they are often skipped in primitive hooking), and they are made up of curved lines like parentheses.

10. Divide the lower quadrant of the face (Line D and below) into thirds (that is, you add two lines within that section: lines E and F). The lips will rest on top of line E.

11. Imagine a line from the center of the pupils to the lipline (Line E); that is how far the child's smile will extend.

12. A mark to indicate the child's chin goes on line F.

13. We usually skip ears; if you put them in, they extend from the middle of the eye (Line A) to Line D.

14. Make the neck as wide as the outside edges of the eyes.

15. If your drawing does not look correct, turn it upside down. You will be better able to locate discrepancies from that angle.

16. Be aware that the following features are often left off primitive children's faces: nostrils, bottom eyelids, ears, and cheeks.

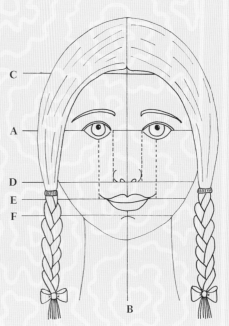

It is interesting—though not surprising—

how many first rugs are of animals.

Hooking Pets and Other Animals

You only have to go to one rug hooking show (held at most rug camps) and see that easily half the rugs are of animals to get this picture: People love their animals and love to hook them. From cows to pigs, to foxes and mice, to deer and moose and, of course, our pet dogs and cats—you'll see them all, again and again, on hooked rugs.

In this respect we are not unlike our ancestors, who also loved to immortalize their animals in wool. Farm animals were always popular—especially sheep, roosters and chickens, and cows and horses. Wild animals—foxes, deer, and bears—show up not uncommonly. And cats seem to have always been beloved of hookers.

(Left) *Jesse's Cat*, hooked by Janet Denlinger from a child's drawing. (Right) Bitty's Wisenbaker's pillow of her dog Peppy.

It's easy to see why. Animals capture the essence of a rug—a familiar, endearing subject that gives us pleasure. Depending upon whom you talk to, hooking animals can be described as easy—or very difficult. Both answers are correct. If you are going for a very realistic look (as, for example in *Eyes and Fur* and *Bonnie's face*), precision and exacting detail are needed, plus finely cut wool. But if you are aiming for a more primitive feel, hooking animals is among the easier and more satisfying of hooking skills, as long as you keep a few central facts in mind:

Keep a visual aid handy and learn to "read" it: A visual aid is a photo or picture of the subject you are hooking. It is invaluable for the details that you

never think about but that can end up making your animal look real. For example, did you know that chickens have yellow eyes? Or that many animals don't have a white portion of the eye?

A generic picture of your breed of dog or cat can work fine for fur color and texture, but to get that face right, use a photo of your pet and keep it right in front of you, where you can refer to it often.

Life in the Country, hooked by Barbara Moran (Keepsake Pattern, available from Harry M. Fraser).

(Left) *Eyes and Fur* sampler, hooked by Sue Hamer, adapted from Jane Flynn pattern. (Right) To get the kind of detail that I achieved in hooking my husband's dog Bonnie, take a close-up photograph of your pet and refer to it frequently.

The simplest animal eyes are just dots, created from one loop and two tails, as in *Cherries and Sheep*, hooked by Celia Leckerman, designed by Marion Ham.

Learn to hook good eyes: The eyes have it, with animals. Hook them first. The simplest—and often, most effective—eyes are just dots, composed of a couple loops (or one loop and two tails), such as used in Celia Leckerman's sheep eyes in *Cherries and Sheep*. Using a strand of black-and-white check can create a lovely eye—seeming to catch "the spark." Some teachers suggest pulling a piece of white cotton thread up into the black pupil, knotting it, and clipping it; this, too, gives a glimmer to the eye that is amazingly lifelike. After hooking the eye, hook around it to contain it.

Use "directional" hooking: After outlining your animal, you hook it in the direction of its fur or feathers. You never hook animals in straight lines, because fur does not grow that way. "Hook along the back as if you are stroking the animal," as Martha Morris poetically phrases it. Sherrie Hieber Day also taught me to think of the muscles and movement of an animal and hook to suggest these also, linking one section to the next with a particular piece of wool.

Marie, hooked by Linda Stutz, is a magnificent example of directional hooking of fur. (Pattern: Yankee Peddler.)

"Hook along the back as if you are stroking the animal."

–MARTHA MORRIS

Use a lot of textured materials: A variety of closely colored, textured wools works best to create the illusion of fur.

Create highlights: Using darker or more textured woolens, add wool highlights to the fur. You can add these first, for primitive rugs, or as you go along, for finer tapestry. Mary Mann's *Fox (below)* is a beautiful example of highlighted fur.

Try to capture expression: If you can capture your animal's expression, your rug will look like your pet. Note how Beth Robison has captured her cat's curiosity in *Parsley in the Lariope*, and Phyllis Silverthorn has conveyed Sam-Mule's placid nature. Both of these rugs, incidentally, are first rugs. (It's interesting—

(Far left) Use a variety of textures and link them, like muscles, in your animal, as in this detail from *Abram's Creek Stag*, hooked by Anne Mather, designed by Bett McLean. (Left) Mary Mann's original *Fox* is a beautiful example of highlighted fur.

(Far left) *Airedale* gets its lifelikeness from the variety of closely colored, textured fabrics Jan Robinson used. (Designed by Sue Hamer and Jan Robinson). (Left) Original first rugs by Beth Robison's *Parsley in the Lariope*.

(Right) First rug *Sam-Mule* by Phyllis Silverthorn. (Far right) *Sammy / Black and Tan*, hooked by Sarah Owens, based on original design "Houndog" [sic] by Mike Segal. Used with permission.

(Left) *Snakes*, hooked and designed by Sarah Owens. (Right) *Fish*, hooked and designed by Pat Tritt.

but perhaps not surprising—how many first rugs are of animals.) And I feel I *know* the black-and-tan *Sammy*.

I don't want to leave you with the impression that all animal rugs are of pets or farm animals, such as sheep. Fish are a popular theme, for example, and fiber artist Sarah Owens chose snakes for her first foray into rug hooking.

Two rug designers have graciously donated patterns of animals for you to hook. Barbara Brown, owner of Port Primitives in Kennebunkport, Maine, created the *Tulip* rug for our book. Patsy Becker, the Cape Cod owner of Patsy B's Creations, gave us one of her most popular patterns —*Annie's Ponies*. (See Projects and Patterns section.) Have fun adapting them.

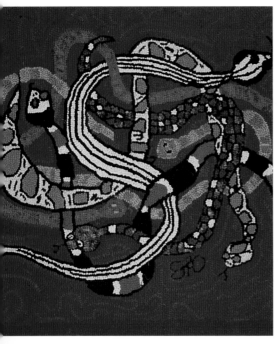

Story of a Rug: *Scrap Cats*

Many a rug hooker refers to the creation of her rug as a "labor of love." But for Katie Puckett and her mother, Michigan rug hooker and teacher Judy Colley, this phrase is not a metaphor. This mother and daughter "teamed up" to create their one-of-a-kind rug, *Scrap Cats*, while awaiting the birth of Katie's second child.

Judy created the cat template (same for all four cats) and drew off a simple 40-inch-by-70-inch pattern on monk's cloth. It basically consisted of two cats per side, "floating on the blank cloth," with only starting and ending lines marked. Then Judy scrounged through her supplies, pulling out plaids for the cats and a variety of mostly pink and purple wools for the background.

"This rug was truly made from scraps," says Judy. Then she packed everything up and went to Florida to await the birth of Katie's child, due in one week.

Judy and Katie set up their Pilgrim frames in the middle of Katie's living room. Facing each other on their chairs, they just started hooking—on different ends of the same rug. The hookers started with the same colors and generally hooked the same palate, checking with each other as they hooked and talked—and awaited labor. The baby was a week late, so they got a lot of hooking in.

"One of us would say, 'What you are doing now?'" Judy recalled. "Then the other would say, 'OK, I'll do that too.'" After doing about 10 rows, they would move the monk's cloth to another position. It took about three moves to get across the width of the 40-inch rug.

They hooked with size 8-cut wool—a first for Judy. "I've been hooking for 28 years, but I'm not a primitive hooker," she admits.

After Marian's birth and before going back to work, Katie went to Michigan to visit her mother, bringing the baby and the rug along. The two women hooked together for another week, taking turns holding the baby while the other caught up. They continued in this fashion "until our frames bumped together," Judy says, laughing. Katie then finished off the rug once at home, where it now graces the front hallway.

Close-up from *Scrap Cats*, hooked by Katie Puckett and her mother, Judy Colley.

The cardinal rule of personalized rug hooking is: Keep it simple.

Houses and Landscapes

Home is where the heart is, the old saw says, and for hookers it is certainly true. Houses of every shape have been the mainstay of hooked rugs for two centuries.

Houses are also relatively straightforward to hook: they're mostly straight lines, and because so many patterns feature houses, they are an ideal place to begin to personalize a pattern. You can buy a house pattern, coloring it in your home's colors and adding your house's defining archi-

tectural nooks and crannies. Then you can landscape it accordingly.

That's what Lee Anderson did with her *Sticky Wicket* rug, a Pat Hornafius pattern distributed by Fraser & Co. Lee was attracted to the pattern because the house on the pattern resembled her Williamsburg colonial. The six cats on the border sealed the deal: Lee has six cats herself. (Incidentally, Fraser has donated this pattern for this book so that others can try personalizing a house rug; or the pattern can be ordered with modifications. See the Patterns and Projects

Lee Anderson personalized Pat Hornafius's *Sticky Wicket* pattern so that it resembled her Williamsburg colonial. (Pattern available from Harry M. Fraser and given at back of this book).

Section.) Nora Findley, likewise, substituted her home in Joan Moshimer's pattern *December Snows*, creating this wonderful winter scene—a not uncommon site in the foothills of Tiger Mountain, Georgia, where Nora lives.

If you want to hook a particular house—yours, the family homestead—have a photo of it handy as a visual aid. But remember the cardinal rule of personalized hooking: Keep it simple. Weed out minor details and emphasize defining elements, such as log and chinking on a log home and adding a brightly colored door on any house. A loop or two will suggest a lantern, for example.

As Chicago artist and rug-hooking teacher Sandy Gannett phrased it, "Use just a whisper of a small line to suggest a window pane, a line or two of color to suggest bricks. You don't want to draw in every brick or stone." Below are some other general suggestions on hooking houses:

Roofs: Outline; fill in with directional hooking—either diagonally or horizontally. Always use texture, such as a tweed or spot-dye. Solid black will "read" like a hole and just hit you, says Gannett, who created the lovely *Family Rug* depicted here.

Windows and doors: Hook these before the house. Yellow, gray-beige, or anything variegated works well for windows. Again, be careful of colors used off the

(Top) *Family Rug*, hooked and designed by Sandy Gannett. (Bottom) Nora Findley chose Joan Moshimer's pattern *December Snows* to recreate the Findleys' Tiger Mountain home.

bolt, as they can make too solid a statement. Yellow suggests a light on at night; tweeds can work well for a door.

Houses: Use darker outlines at corners and under the roofline. Hook the sides of the house a shade darker, as if they are in shadows. Hook directionally, usually horizontally for clapboard and log cabins, though some cedar homes and older structures are vertically planked, such as the bridge in Mary Lu Cole's *Covered*

Bridge. For a clapboard, use a good, non-fraying wool with variations in color to suggest age. Never use stark white, even if your house is white. Dye it with very little of another color, such as silver gray or old ivory. Or just throw your white wool in the pot at the tail end of dyeing the related colors in your rug.

Log cabins: You can use different-sized cuts—an 8- or 9-cut for the logs, a 6 for the chinking. And in this case, *don't* pull

(Right) Hooking the chinking in a log cabin in a smaller cut than the logs adds verisimilitude. Rug: *Log Cabin,* hooked by Anne Mather, designed by Patsy Becker. From the collection of Mary Virginia Davis.

the chinking color up to be even to the surrounding loops; it will look more realistic. Tweeds or spot-dyes work equally well, as long as you get texture.

Landscapes: Sandy Gannett also has several excellent suggestions for landscaping in your rug. The first, again, is to simplify. You can't put in every bush, so "prune" them down. Pick out the defining, major elements in your yard and emphasize them. "If I had put every tree and shrub in my yard, you wouldn't have even been able to see the house," says Gannett. "Keep to your focus"—in her case, the house.

Similarly, in *Dad's Home (below)*, I emphasized only two trees, an ivy patch, and ubiquitous dandelions, even though the home has an elaborately landscaped yard.

Second, feel free to move things around, to shorten a yard, drop a part of the house or roof—whatever is necessary to improve your design.

Third, put more texture in the front of your rug and "wash out" the background. For example, in Gannett's rug, the trees in back are actually hooked in a textured gray, whereas in front, trees and shrubs have a lot of green variegation and color. Similarly, in Mary Lu Cole's *Covered Bridge*, notice the intensity of the tree detail and foreground, but faintly visible church steeple in the back. Playing with detail this way adds perspective, verisimilitude, and depth to your rug.

(Above) Gannett's *Family Rug* illustrates adding foreground texture and "washing out" the background. (Below) Simplify landscaping, even when the house belongs to a landscape architect, as was the case in *Dad's Home*, hooked and designed by Anne Mather for her brother David's family.

DAD'S HOME!

Tips on Hooking Skies

Many rug hookers find skies a particular challenge. Since Sandy Gannett's gorgeous sky was the first thing I noticed in her *Family Rug*, I asked her to share some of her tips. Here are her suggestions:

- Hook skies straight across, but hook clouds circularly.

- Hook the sky darker at the top of your rug and lighter at the horizon.

- To get a subtle sky, marry together combinations of blues, grays, and naturals in detergent without bleach. When you're happy with the color, pull the wool out and transfer it to another steaming pot with vinegar.

Detail of sky from Gannett's *Family Rug*.

- Gannett's friend and fellow hooking teacher Sue Hamer suggests dividing your wool for the sky into two batches. Dye one batch in the formula you've chosen; dye the second in the same formula, diluted one-half strength. Then use the lighter color on the horizon and work up to the darker. Sue has an additional spin on this formula: Make a third batch, diluted one-fourth. Use it for the clouds.

Borders on House Rugs

House rugs are a good place for thematic borders. In Gannett's *Family Rug*, for example, the artist put meaningful family symbols of her husband and children. Here again, though, she had to simplify, which in this case meant not trying to squeeze memories of the grandchildren in too. It would have become too busy.

Pat Tritt, in her *Camellia House* rug, chose the perfect theme for her borders: over 300 of these lovely plants surround her son's home, which is depicted in the rug.

Sometimes, however, a house rug can just be too busy to support a thematic, similarly busy border. This is true for many pictorial-style rugs, such as Beverly Goodrich's *Memories on the Farm*. Beverly chose a simple, framed border. Some pictorials have no border at all.

One final note about borders: As a general rule, don't introduce a new color in the border. However, you can go a shade darker. In Gannett's rug, for example, the yellow in the border is a shade darker than that used in the house.

(Above) Pat Tritt chose—what else?—camellias for her border on *Camellia House*, her hooked tribute to her son's home. (Below) Simple borders often work best on pictorial-style rugs, such as *Memories on the Farm*, an original by Beverly Goodrich.

Story of a Rug: *Bottom Star–Big Dipper*

By Stephanie Krauss

AUTHOR'S NOTE: *About 6 months before I began writing this book, my teacher and good friend Mary Williamson handed me a photo of a rug that a student had given her. The photo haunted both of us. When I got the contract for this book, I started to search in earnest for the creator of this rug—my only clues, "SAK," the initials in the corner. I called every rug hooker with those initials in the ATHA national directory, to no avail. Then, while talking to designer Patsy Becker, I mentioned the rug. She was going to a national ATHA conference soon, she said; why didn't I fax her a photograph of the rug? So I made up a flier and faxed it to her. The next day Patsy called. "You better sit down," she said. And once I heard the rug's story, I knew why it had haunted Mary and me, and why it needed to be in this book.*

February 12, 1998, is a day that will live in infamy—at least in my family. That was the day my husband, Clint, was diagnosed with terminal cancer of the liver. Our doctor left little doubt about the finality, predicting the end in four to six months, perhaps as few as two months. My husband walked out of the doctor's office on that sunny afternoon and swung into action in his usual calm and organized manner. He contacted our local hospice organization, consulted with a grief counselor, and called his boss at the Vermont Department of Motor Vehicles to begin the process of separating from his job. He organized our legal and financial affairs and researched all the possibilities for future state and federal entitlements. I, too, was caught up in the initial surge of action. I called the school guidance counselors, teachers, my extended family, and even a personal therapist for myself.

During the first weeks, we tackled the tasks of organizing our life with great energy, love, support, and even a strange peace, but as the weeks wore on and the tasks were completed, we sagged into a kind of stupor. All the members of my family stopped doing what they usually do. Clint stopped reading and collecting books. The phone stopped ringing for our teenagers and I stopped hooking.

We reached one of our lowest moments one Sunday afternoon about six weeks after the diagnosis. We were standing in the kitchen, hugging, when I finally broke down and sobbed, "What am I going to do without you?" Quietly, Clint said, "Don't worry. I'll always be with you. I'll be on the bottom star of the Big Dipper." I clung to him, repeating, "Bottom star, Big Dipper, bottom star, Big Dipper. I'll never remember that." Throughout the day, I kept repeating it like a mantra and later, I went to bed still worrying that I would forget Clint's words. Sometime in the night I realized that I needed some kind of a touchstone to remind me. Then I dreamed of a rug. I woke up thinking, "I am a rug hooker. That is what I do." My touchstone was clear.

The length of the words together would determine the size of my new rug. On a large piece of paper I placed the letters and started to sketch the beginnings of a picture. I worked at the dining room table, drawing the details of our house, the mountains, and the constellation. As time passed, each one of my daughters wandered through the room and watched as I drew. My oldest daughter helped straighten the perspective of the house. With rule and pencil, she added her suggestions. Next, my middle daughter explained that the Big Dipper is only visible during the winter months, so the mountains should be snow-covered. We discussed how that might look and decided that the green leafy things in the corner of the rug wouldn't be appropriate, even if this is Vermont with all its

Bottom Star–Big Dipper, hooked and designed by Stephanie Krauss. Photograph by Ed Wissner.

peculiar weather. At just that moment, my youngest daughter happened to pass by. She chimed in that evergreens were green all the time, so why not make them pine trees? My picture—our picture—was coming together. Some days later, when I was about to transfer the picture to the backing, Clint stood contemplating the design. "I think there needs to be a moon," he said. So I added a moon.

As the picture progressed through printing, color planning, dyeing, and hooking, it became apparent that we were all starting to move again in our normal patterns. Clint read and again searched for books to add to his antiquarian book collection. Our teenagers were, again, constantly on the phone, and I was hooking. There is comfort in the routines of life.

Clint and I spent the summer and early fall mostly outside on the porch. The weather was glorious and the birds sang. Clint read and slept, and I kept hooking. We talked, planned, dreamed, remembered…and started to say goodbye. I finished the rug in September. Clint died October 15, 1998.

AUTHOR'S NOTE CONTINUED: *It is no surprise that this rug became the vehicle it did. Women have used hooked rugs to express their feelings for over a century. Marriages, births, places, and favorite pets were commemorated in hooked rugs. Coffin rugs were a part of funeral services in the 1800s. Women hooked their thoughts about religion, politics, and even family members. Bottom Star–Big Dipper is a memorial to Clint and to an incredible family journey filled with deep sadness and great joy of life.*

Stephanie promised herself when Clint died that within the next year she would chronicle this journey. When I called her on October 15, 1999—one year to the day that Clint had died—we both knew that her story was meant to be in this book.

Pulling It All Together:
The Story Rug

Betty Laine's rendition of Jane Flynn's pattern *Gabbeh* (available from Charco Patterns).

As is certainly clear to you by now, rug hookers like to tell stories, their rugs often tell stories, and hookers even like to tell stories about their rugs! So I guess it was inevitable that "story rugs" would emerge on the scene. In a sense, of course, every rug has a story. But story rugs are more like samplers in wool: they combine many motifs to capture a person's—or even a town's—life story.

The customary basis for story rugs is the "azeri," the now trademarked name for a woven Turkish folk carpet recently popularized in the book *AZERI™ Folklife Carpets* (Woven Legends, 1992). These large, primitive Orientals, which depict life in the village of the weavers creating them, are now desirable decorating items.

Rug designers are now offering Azeri™-style rugs. They have a very distinctive style. Elaborate, oriental-style borders encase the body of the rug. Small motifs and flowers (called "beads," and meant, in the original Turkish rugs, to ward off evil) dot the pattern. To imitate the woven look, all hooking except for the pictures within the rug is done straight across, usually in a 5- or 6-cut or smaller. To capture the oriental flavor,

the main color palette is limited to three colors plus a neutral. A jeweled spot-dye is used for outlining. An example of one popular Azeri™ pattern, Jane Flynn's *Gabbeh*, is shown opposite. (Of interest to rug hookers, there is even a story rug, *Folklife Oriental*, designed by Ingrid Hieronimus, available from Canada's Ragg Tyme Studio.)

But what's really fun is that now hookers are *personalizing* such patterns. In Connie Hughes's brilliantly colored version of Flynn's *Gabbeh* pattern, for example, she exchanged the camels for her husband's antique cars! In the body of water, she dropped the fish from the pattern and substituted herself and family members, decked out in bathing caps.

Similarly, Faith Williston adapted Jane Flynn's new pattern, *East Meets*

Connie Hughes's adaptation of *Gabbeh*.

East Meets West, hooked by Faith Williston, adapted from Jane Flynn's new pattern of the same name (available from Charco).

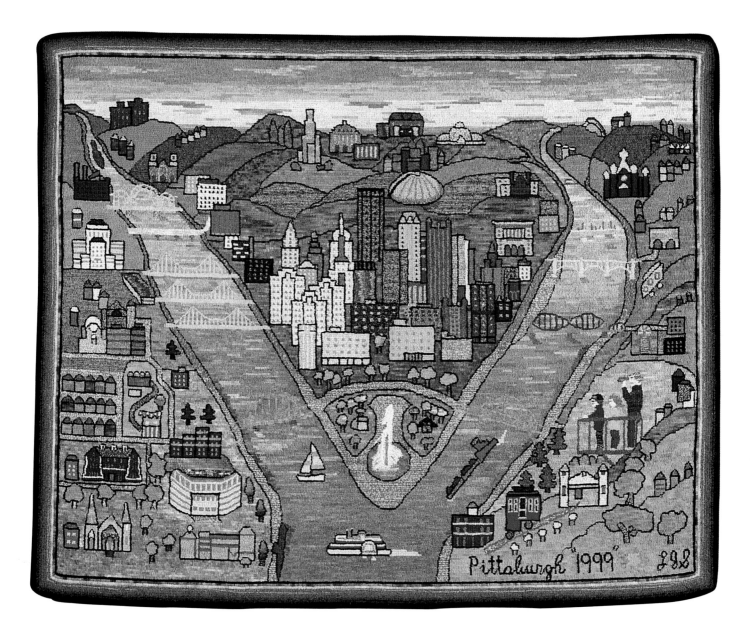

West, to create a rug to honor a dear friend who had died. The different scenes depict memory-filled sights in Washington, D.C., and Mount Vernon—and commemorate their mutual fondness for rug hooking!

If you want to adapt an existing pattern, talk to your rug designer. Both Charlotte Price (distributor of Jane Flynn's patterns) and Pris Buttler (with several Azeri™-style patterns available) will leave the centers of these patterns blank. This way, the complicated border is done and you have a head start on designing the fun part.

Or you can design your own rug from scratch. That's what the members of the Pittsburgh Rug Hooking Guild did to create their mural-like piece, *Pittsburgh*. "Everyone added their say, their favorite part of the city," says member Connie Hughes. The group-designed rug was then hooked by a single member, Lois Sherwood.

This Azeri™ -styled tribute to the city of Pittsburgh was hooked by Lois Sherwood but designed by all the members of the Pittsburgh Rug Hooking Guild.

Greenwich Village storefront. Think symbols, and think simple.

Places you live include not just states or countries, but your homes along the way. You can hook your favorite houses, the stream you lived near as a child, a mountain retreat you love. Your personal geography, in fact, will likely create the backbone of the rug: the trees you choose, the lakes, the roads. Think about what you love about a place and list it.

Similarly, you will want to represent people and pets. The latter can be easy; the former may not be. Thus, some people put few figures and more symbols of those people: a guitar for a guitarist, a water hole to denote swimming. You can't put your whole childhood in a rug, but you can, as Faith Williston did, suggest a happy childhood—with children jumping rope.

Now start assembling pictures of the places, people, and pets you've listed. You can use magazines to supplement your photos, or images from coloring books. Or, if you're skilled at drawing, you can sketch them.

When you have twenty or so pictures for your rug, you need to start thinking about an overall design. As with a sampler, there need not be a particular order to the items—they can just float in the background wool. But usually you will want some tie that binds: a road, perhaps, or a river. A family tree can be very effective.

Or, you may want to divide the rug into sections for different periods of your life. This is commonly done in Turkish rugs. Rebecca Knudsen organized her mother's story rug, *Mom Burch*, around

Mom Burch, hooked and designed by Rebecca Knudsen.

Designing the Story Rug

Whether you "edit" an existing pattern or create a story rug from scratch, the process is very similar. Basically, you do an inventory of your life. What are some major life events (births, weddings, accomplishments)? Who are some treasured people? In what places have you loved living? What are your hobbies, your loves?

Now you translate this inventory into pictures. Think metaphorically. For example, if you once lived in Georgia, you can draw a map of that state—or you can simply add a peach. New York City can be the Empire State Building—or a

her mother, with details of her life floating around her. Pat Tritt's story rug *Patrick's World* depicts the personal geography of her son's life.

As mentioned above, orientals have a stricter color plan than any other type of hooked rug. Basically, they use the three primary colors—red, blue, and yellow (gold)—and a neutral, such as a cream or parchment color. You dye two or three shades of each of these four colors. For example, shades of red would be brick, rust, and rose. Shades of blue would be navy, pale blue, and turquoise. You also need an outline color. Often this is a colorful spot-dye that adds "poison" and interest. It is used to outline every single motif of the rug. Orientals use green very sparingly because it is considered a holy color, mainly used for prayer rugs. Black, which was hard to dye, is also avoided. Brown may be used for animals.

Orientals—and thus Azeris™—are characterized by a variegated streaking caused by the dyeings' being done at different watering holes. Modern hookers approximate this effect by abrashing, a method of dyeing multiple values on one piece of wool. For Pro-Chem dyes, a good source for dyeing formulas and methods for oriental rugs is the $6 paperback pamphlet *Prisms I* by Claire deRoos and Nancy MacLennan, which has 35 formulas for orientals. For Cushing dyes, a good source is the $7 paperback *Scraps and Spots: 115 Formulas for Rug Hooking* by Dotti Ebi. Both are widely available from hooking supply sources.

In your creation of a personal story rug, I hope you enjoy your "journey." Perhaps the defining element of these rugs, as Charlotte Price says, is that they are "full of joy." Looking at the examples here, who can disagree?

Patrick's World, Pat Tritt's story rug about her son's life.

"My paintings are my memories."

—MARC CHAGALL

Unusual Uses for Hooking

You are probably wondering what you will do when you run out of wall or floor space for your many rugs. If you're a beginner, you really don't need to worry about this for a while, trust me. But eventually you will start to wonder where you will fit all your beloved hooked pieces. Well, hooking isn't just for rugs anymore. Hookers are now, among other things, wearing their art.

Hooking on wool can create a gorgeous vest, for example. Shown are several examples hooked by students of Mary Williamson. Mark off, with chalk or a basting stitch, the front panel of your vest (or whatever portion you plan to hook). Hook it before you cut out the pattern pieces; this ensures you have enough fabric to grip in your hook or frame. Once you've completed your hooking, cut out the pieces and assemble your vest as indicated in the directions for the project.

Hooking can also be used for purses, and for pins such as the darling pumpkin pin created by Linda Mather, above opposite. Hooked Christmas ornaments

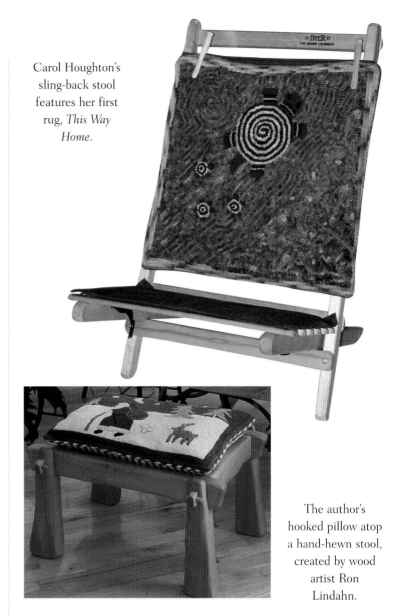

Carol Houghton's sling-back stool features her first rug, *This Way Home*.

can be treasured gifts. When creating pins or ornaments, draw off several on your background fabric and hook them all before proceeding. Then cut close to the hooking; apply a product that stops fraying; and glue on a felt backing. For a pin, add a safety pin; for an ornament, glue in a looped piece of ribbon between the felt and the hooking, for hanging.

Speaking of holiday crafts, many rug enthusiasts, such as Tennessee veteran hooker Maryon Clonts and her daughter-in-law Rose Fiumara, have used the craft to create Christmas stockings for family members. See samples shown below.

Hooking can also enhance a piece of furniture, particularly stools. Here are several examples—a sling-back, a pillow on a hand-hewn stool, and a cover commissioned for a large, upholstered stool. Note that when you create a hooked cover for a stool with a high rise, you should leave the corners unhooked so that the upholsterer can tidily tuck in the corners. Many designers create stool

The author's hooked pillow atop a hand-hewn stool, created by wood artist Ron Lindahn.

A hooked pin (above) makes a nice gift…as do Christmas stockings.

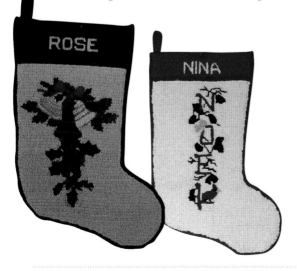

Cat in the Bird House, an original commissioned by Maggie and Bob Hatcher, demonstrates how to hook an upholstered piece: leave mitered, blank corners so that the finished stool cover will have smooth corners. Rug by Anne Mather.

Southwestern Santa, hooked by Anne Mather, designed by Janet Dobson (Sweet Briar Studio).

Pat Tritt's slickered fisherman was adapted from a Janet Dobson pattern.

covers and piano seat covers, or you can create your own. Hooked chair pads and table mats are two other popular uses for this fiber art, ones that enhance the patina of the furniture they cover.

Some designers also feature hooked figures, such as *Southwestern Santa* shown here. This is just one of numerous unusual Santas created by designer Janet Dobson (Sweet Briar Studio). Finishing directions are included with each pattern. The same patterns can be altered for year-round enjoyment. For example, Atlanta artist Pat Tritt has created a fisherman in a yellow slicker from a Santa figure pattern.

Pat also has a couple of other unusual uses for hooking. She has taken drawings by her grandchildren and hooked them as pillows. She has even mounted

a hooked rug on a firescreen, created by her husband Bob and stenciled by Pat. Speak of an heirloom!

And Pris Buttler, the award-winning rug hooker/designer from Gainesville, Georgia, has created several doll patterns with hooked faces and feet. These copyrighted patterns come with detailed directions and fabric for outfits to dress the dolls.

Finally, you can create mini hooked rugs. Little Quilts, an Atlanta quilt-designing company and hooking/quilting center, publishes patterns for mini-rugs. They make lovely table mats or wall hangings. Chicago designer Sue Hamer has created two mini pieces suitable for table mats or trivets. Her patterns and the instructions for making them are given in the Projects and Patterns section.

Pris Buttler has created several doll patterns with hooked faces and feet. Pictured, from left to right, are *Chad*, red-headed *Paige*, *Phillip*, and *Lindsey*.

Projects
and Patterns

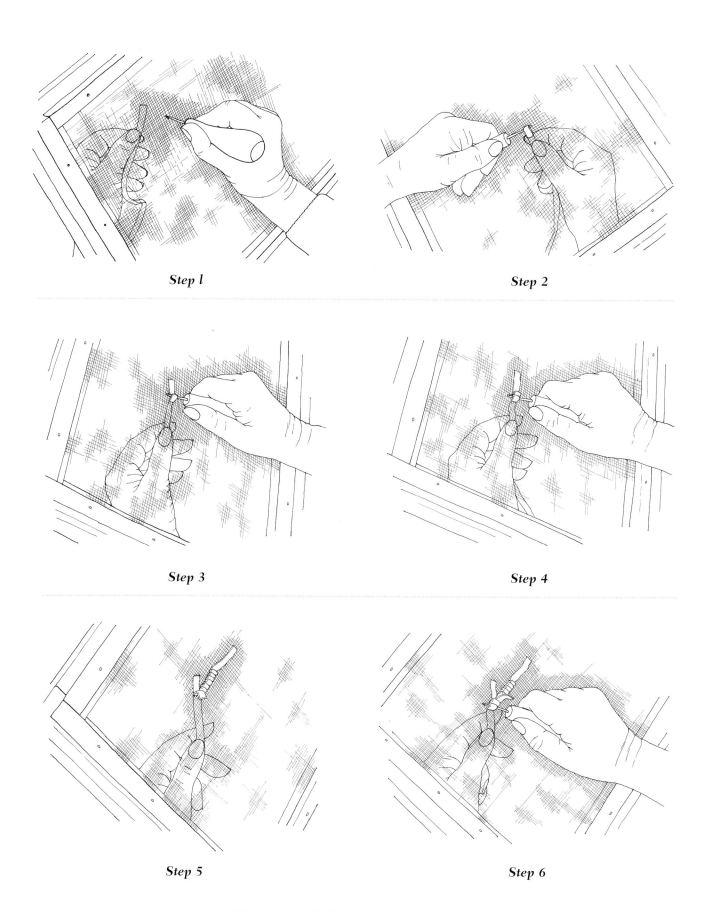

Step 1

Step 2

Step 3

Step 4

Step 5

Step 6

Art by Tom Mather, *The Art of Rug Hooking* (Sterling, 1998). Reproduced with permission.

General Directions

How to Hook

Rug hooking is done on a frame or hoop, which can either be set on your lap or mounted on a stand. Stretch your background fabric (burlap, linen, monk's cloth, or rug warp) on the frame.

Your hooking tool is called a hook; it resembles a crochet hook mounted in wood or plastic. You hook with woolen cloth, ideally flannel weight, cut into strips of varying width. For fine hooking, you use thin strips (e.g., $\frac{3}{32}$nd- or $\frac{5}{32}$nd-cuts, commonly called 3-cut and 5-cut, referring to the cutting wheel that automatically creates strips of this width). Cutters are available from Harry M. Fraser or your local rug-hooking supply or quilt store. Wide-cut strips generally measure $\frac{1}{4}$ inch (an 8-cut). One can also hand-cut or use a rotary cutter. Hand-cut wool often is up to $\frac{1}{2}$-inch wide.

The technique of rug hooking consists of basically one stitch. This stitch is depicted in the 6 steps at left. These illustrations feature a see-through screen where the burlap or background fabric would be.

Step 1: Insert your hook, open side at about a 10-o'clock position. Hold your wool strip in your other (usually left) hand and poise it to the left of the hook.

Step 2: With the hook, catch the wool from behind, creating a loop. Pull this loop through your fabric.

Step 3: Pull your first loop all the way through, creating a "tail." You have a tail at the beginning and end of every strip. Always pull your tails to the top of your work. Later, you trim these off. After creating your tail, repeat steps 1 and 2 to create another loop. Create this second stitch in the hole immediately adjacent to your tail.

Step 4: Reinsert the empty hook through the fabric to the left of your first loop. Do not pack it into the very next hole; leave a space or two, depending upon how wide your strip is. Pull the loop up through the fabric to a height equal to the last stitch. Your loops should be approximately as high as they are wide. Thus, an 8-cut ($\frac{1}{4}$-inch wide) should be pulled up $\frac{1}{4}$ inch.

Step 5: Continue creating loops until your strip ends. Pull the tail up through the top. Pull the tail from your next strip of wool up through the same hole as the ending tail of your last strip of wool.

Step 6: Repeat this process of creating loops until you have covered the area of your rug that you want to be of a certain color. You may hook straight across (usually towards you, that is, from right to left, or top to bottom) or in swirls. Do not try to hook in every hole or your rug will not lie flat. However, never let the background fabric show through from the top.

How to Draw Out Patterns

There are dozens of talented rug designers with catalogs of rug designs. So the simplest method of obtaining a pattern is to buy one directly from a designer or purchase one at a rug camp, through a teacher, or from a quilting or hooking supply store. Designers are advertised in the *Newsletter of Association of Traditional Hooking Artists* (ATHA) and in *Rug Hooking* magazine.

If you create your own pattern, draw it first on a large sheet of paper, or assemble small parts or templates and move them around on a large sheet of paper until you're happy with the layout. Then glue-stick them down. Next, trace this draft pattern onto "red-dot" pattern tracing material (available from any large fabric store) with a permanent marker. Finally, lay the red-dot pattern onto your background fabric and secure it with pins or tape; using your permanent marker again, press down through the red-dot, which is porous enough to allow the ink to seep through to your pattern. You may need to go over some lines, once you have removed the red-dot. Now zig-zag around the outside of your border, about ¼ inch from the edge. Also zigzag the raw edges of the background material (or put masking tape on it) to keep the edges from fraying.

A third way to obtain a pattern is to copy an established design, such as those at the back of this book, donated by designers. These need to be enlarged and traced onto your background fabric of burlap, linen, monk's cloth, or rug warp. You can enlarge it by using an overhead projector. Once you have it on a large sheet of paper, copy it to red-dot and then to your background fabric, as indicated above.

These are the basic steps of rug hooking and preparing a fabric for rug hooking. For more detailed instructions about dyeing, finishing, purchasing wool, and related subjects, please see my first book, *The Art of Rug Hooking* (Sterling, 1998).

Projects / Patterns / Alphabets

Wool Strip Tote
Designed by Sandy Myers

Create this wonderful tote to store and carry cut wool for your in-progress rug.

Materials

- *½ yard pre-quilted fabric*
- *⅞ yard snap tape (found in drapery department)*
- *2 yards ribbon (¼ or ⅝ inch wide)*
- *1 yard of ¼-inch-wide contrasting cloth, for binding*
- *Pre-quilted fabric cut 26½ by 17½ inches*

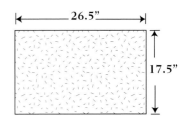

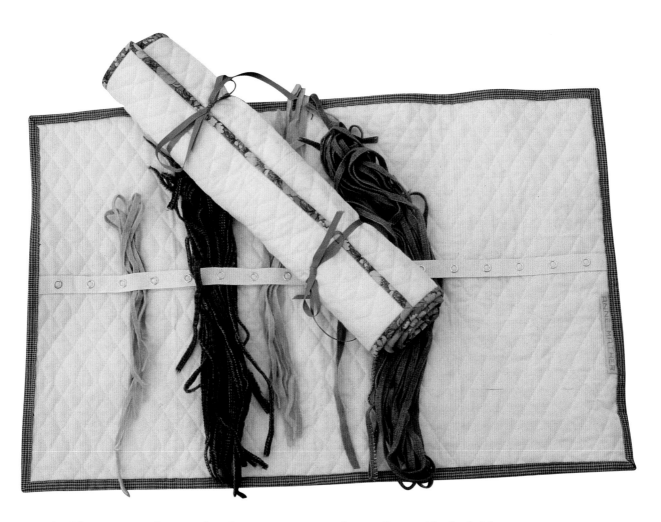

This fabric tote not only carries but also organizes your wool strips. Designed by Sandy Myers.

Instructions

Unsnap tape and sew bottom strip lengthwise to center of tote. When sewn in place, snap top strip of tape to bottom strip. Edges will be sewn in with binding.

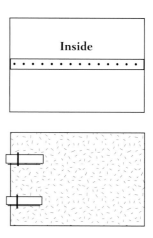

Cut ribbon into four 18-inch lengths. On outer side of tote, layer two ribbon lengths together and pin 3½ inches in from edge, as shown. Ends will be sewn in with binding.

Binding

Cut two binding strips 2¼ inches wide by 44 inches long. Join with diagonal seam to measure 2¼ by 88 inches. Fold the long binding in half lengthwise, with wrong sides together, and press.

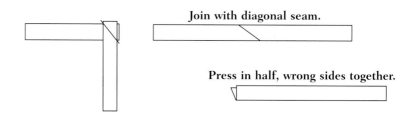

Join with diagonal seam.

Press in half, wrong sides together.

On outside of tote, begin in the middle of a side, not at a corner. Place binding at edge, align raw edges (folded edge of binding to center). Fold over about 1 inch and begin sewing using a ¼-inch seam allowance, about ½ inch from fold.

As you near a corner, stop sewing ¼ inch from the end, back-stitch, and remove tote from machine. Fold binding up at 45° angle then fold back down so a fold is at the upper edge. Resume sewing and repeat at each corner, catching ends of snap tape and ribbons.

To finish binding, overlap folded edge at beginning section and stitch across seam.

Turn binding to inside of tote and slipstitch in place to enclose all raw edges.

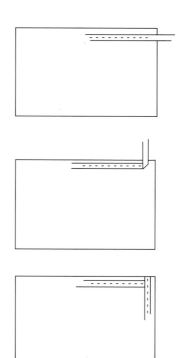

Hooked Trivets: Stars & Fruit

Hooked and designed by Sue Hamer

Table mats are very useful as coasters or trivets. This is a fun beginning project that can be completed in a few evenings.

Mat Size (one)
6½ by 6½ inches

Materials (each mat)
Tracing paper

Waterproof marker

Burlap, linen, or monk's cloth

¼ yard total fabric scraps for each mat, cut into ⅛- to ¼-inch strips

Lining (optional)

Stars, designed and hooked by Sue Hamer.

Fruit, designed and hooked by Sue Hamer.

Instructions

To create a pattern:

1. Using tracing paper and a marker, trace the pattern from the book. Add another line 1½ inches from the outer edge of the design all the way around for your border.

2. Tape the design on a light box or window. Put the burlap on the design and, with the marker, trace onto the burlap.

3. Zigzag the edges to prevent fraying.

To hook Stars:

1. With light wool, hook the outline of the stars. Using another light color, hook the inside of the stars.

2. Using a dark color wool, hook around each star.

3. Hook the outside edge of the piece with one line of dark wool.

4. Fill in the unhooked background with other dark colors.

To hook Fruit:

1. Make a black-and-white photocopy of the colored picture of the *Fruit* trivet.

2. Study the photo to determine where to put your highlights (light colors) and shaded areas (darker wool).

3. With ⅛-inch-wide strips, outline each fruit, beginning with those in the foreground. For the apple outline, for example, use a dark red. For the front pear, use a brownish material for the left side, with a lighter value on the right, as indicated by the photo.

4. Add brown stems.

5. Hook highlights.

6. Hook darkest areas, such as the shadow on the back pear (I used a dark green). With both pictures as your guides and an assortment of colors, fill in between the outlines and highlights and shadows.

7. Hook a "holding line" border with your tabletop color around the entire piece.

8. Outline each fruit with wall color.

9. Hook the tabletop in a horizontal direction.

10. Hook walls in a vertical direction.

Finishing

Steam-press and dry flat. Turn back edge, leaving ¼ inch of burlap showing. Whip this edge with wool yarn to match tabletop color. If you choose to line, cut lining material ¼ inch larger than finished piece. Turn under and sew to back. Press.

The Paper Doll Rug

Rug concept and "Maggie" pattern by Anne Mather
Additional rug designs, dolls and clothes templates by Gail Loder

Detailed instructions on how to trace and enlarge patterns are in the beginning of this section. Also study Sue Hamer's instructions for Hooked Trivets for practical tips.

Instructions on how to adapt doll and clothes templates are in the Creating Your Own Patterns section of the book.

(Above) *Maggie Paper Doll Rug*, hooked and designed by Anne Mather. SIZE: 21.5 by 33 inches.
(Below) *Brooke* paper doll rug, hooked and designed by Gail Loder. SIZE: 22 by 34 inches.

Annie's Ponies

DESIGNER: Patsy Becker. Hooked by Cherylyn Brubaker.
SIZE: 18 by 45 inches

Tulip

DESIGNER: Barbara Brown (Port Primitives). Hooked by Linda Mather.
SIZE: 20⅝ by 25 inches

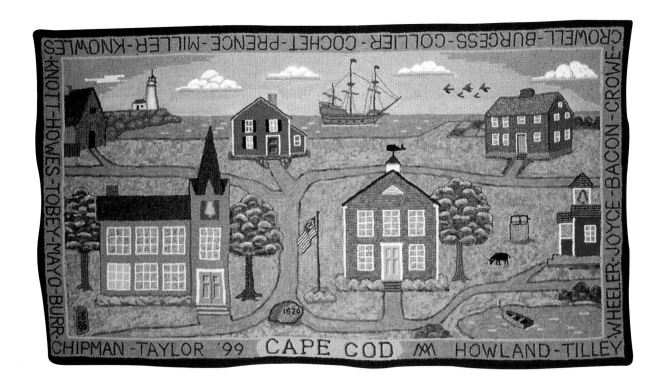

The Village

DESIGNER: Lib Callaway (available from Margaret Siano).
SIZE: 30 by 58 inches

Sticky Wicket

DESIGNER: Pat Hornafius (available from Harry M. Fraser Co.), copyright pre-1993.
Hooked by Lee Anderson. SIZE: 25 by 40 inches

Appalachian Sampler

Hooked and designed by Bett McLean. Copyright 1995. SIZE: 24 by 36 inches

Mille Fleur

DESIGNER: Jane McGown Flynn (available from Charco Patterns). SIZE: 24 by 36 inches

ABCDEEFGHIJKLM
NOPQRSTUVWXYZ
abcdefghijklmnopqrst
uvwxyz1234567890 &

ABCDEEFGHIJKLM
NOPQRSTUVWXYZ
abcdefghijklmnopqrst
uvwxyz1234567890 &

ABCDEEFGHIJKLMNO
PQRSTUVWXYZ
abcdefghijklmnopqrst
uvwxyz1234567890 &

ABCDEFGHIJKLMNOPQ
RSTUVWXYZ
abcdefghijklmnopqrst
uvwxyz1234567890 &

ABCDEFGHIJKM
LNOPQRSTUV
WXYZ 1234567890 &

ABCDEEFGHIJKLM
NOPQRSTUVWXYZ
abcdefghijklmnopqrst
uvwxyz 1234567890 &

About the Hookers

Lee Anderson started hooking after a mother–daughter trip to Nantucket in 1989. Primitives are her favorites, especially ones with a cat in them. She grew up with dogs, cats, and horses and currently has three cats and four "grand-cats" that she has hooked in various rugs. Lee is the mother of three grown children and is a wife of 32 years. She lives in Rocky Mount and Chapel Hill, N.C.

B. J. Andreas is a McGown-certified teacher, residing in Marathon, Florida, who has become known for her bright, bold colors and great love of primitives. She has been teaching for 22 years around the country and in Canada. She has also held many positions with ATHA's Board of Directors, including editor and communications director for 9 years.

Marilyn Bottjer began rug hooking in 1967 and has been teaching private classes since 1972. She teaches at Caraway (Asheboro, N.C.), Highlands (Fort Washington, Pa.), Green Mountain (Vt.), and ATHA rug camps. She also teaches workshops at the Museum of American Folk Art in New York City and the Brookfield Craft Center in Brookfield, Conn. Her work has been featured in numerous juried exhibits. She is an accredited McGown teacher.

Cherylyn Brubaker is married to a retired naval officer, Thomas, and now resides in Brunswick, Me. She earned an art degree in 1975. Over the years in their many duty assignments, she was employed in the graphic arts field. Since settling down in Maine and being introduced to rug hooking in 1994, rug hooking has taken on a life of its own! Between squiring two active boys, Nick and Tim, Cherylyn has her own rug-hooking business, Hooked Treasures. She designs patterns, teaches classes, and is a co-director of the Maine Coast Rug Camp. This year she and her sister, Terri Quinn, took over Heirloom Rugs. Cherylyn's hooked rugs have been displayed at the Wenham Museum in Wenham, Mass., and the Brick Store Museum in Kennebunkport, Me, and have appeared in *Rug Hooking* magazine.

Pris Buttler is a folk artist/rug hooker who began her own line of patterns for rug hookers in 1999. Her paintings sell in Timpson Creek Gallery (Clayton, Ga.) and hang in the House of Blue (Walt Disney World, Fla., and Myrtle Beach, S.C.). She placed as a finalist in an *Artists Magazine* 1998 competition featuring 9,000 artists worldwide. Her works hang in Sapporo, Japan; Georgia's ex-Gov. Zell Miller's home; and the Air and Space Smithsonian Museum, Washington, D.C., among others. Her rug *Our Captain Stood* was featured in *Rug Hooking* magazine's Celebrations VIII and was chosen third place for original design. She also won an award of excellence at Sauder Village (Archbold, Ohio) in 1999 for her rug *The Whole Week's Picking*. She teaches lettering and design for rug hooking and has a pamphlet, "Lettering Tips for the Rug Hooker," and a pattern catalog, "Something for Everyone 2." She was also featured in Anne Mather's *The Art of Rug Hooking.*

Pat Chancey is a retired librarian and high school English teacher. A mother of two boys—and a grandmother—she lives with her husband in Dallas, Tex. Pat became interested in rug hooking through her mother and has been teaching for 25 years. A certified McGown teacher, she is active in Southeastern Teachers' Workshop, was a charter member of Western Teachers' Workshop, and began teacher-training at North Teachers' Workshop in 1980. She has been Director of Texas Rug Camp since 1990 and has taught at other rug schools and camps, such as Caraway, Sebring, Fla., and ATHA Biennial (Bend, Oregon). Pat is a member of ATHA (board member and Exhibit Chairman of the 1995 Biennial in Arlington, Tex.) and the International Guild of Handhooking Rugmakers; and is now Director of South Central McGown Teachers' Workshop, which will begin in North Texas in the year 2000.

Maryon Clonts is a retired university math professor and the former "Number Lady", who taught elementary math on public television in Tennessee. She now lives in Andersonville, Tenn. She has one son and two stepchildren and enjoys hooking rugs for her grandchildren. Her work was also featured in *The Art of Rug Hooking.*

Mary Lu Cole, raised in Michigan, is a retired Air Force lieutenant colonel who served as a psychiatric nurse. She lives in the mountains in Rabun Gap, Ga. Her work has been widely exhibited, is in many private collections, and was featured in *The Art of Rug Hooking.*

Judy Colley You know the saying, "The first day of the rest of your life"? That was the day Judy first saw traditional rug hooking being done at the Michigan state fair. Once she found a teacher, the craft quickly became and has continued to be a large part of her life. She has been rug hooking for 28 years and teaching for 25. Her daughter Katie now joins her in hooking and running a rug school, On the Ocean Rug Hooking Conference, which met in Jacksonville, Fla., in January 2000. She also teaches classes in her Michigan home and at other rug schools. Her interest is in all different aspects of rug hooking, but mostly color and dyeing. She teaches because she believes that "everyone should have the opportunity to create something beautiful and lasting and that rug hooking meets those requirements."

Marguerite Culberson is an artist and homemaker living in Lawrenceville, Ga., with her husband, Rick, and two children, Matthew and McKenzie. Her first rug was featured in *The Art of Rug Hooking.*

Janet Denlinger, a biochemist, is a co-founder and Executive Vice President of Biomatrix, Inc., a biotechnology company that develops and manufactures elastoviscous medical therapeutic devices. She has been hooking since 1992, and divides her time and her supplies of wool and hooking equipment between the United States and France.

Trudy DuVerger is originally from Worcester, Mass., where she was an interior decorator. She now lives in Waynesville, N.C. She has been hooking for only one year. *Woodland Adventure*, her first rug, was hooked for her son and only child, Roy Jr. She is now designing a *Woodland Adventure II* for her husband, Roy. Although Trudy is self-taught, she has some wonderful hooking friends who are more than generous with their hooking knowledge.

Mary Evans has been hooking with friends for about 14 years. She was an art major at Agnes Scott College, so she likes to design her own rugs. She has been married to Coley Evans for 40 years, is the mother of three grown sons, and is a grandmother as well. She and her husband live in Atlanta and also enjoy spending a lot of time at Lake Rabun in North Georgia.

Nora Findley is a nurse who was raised in the Northeast, but now makes her home in the North Georgia mountains. She's raising two children with her husband and has been enjoying rug hooking for 11 years. She enjoys both the creativity of the craft and the camaraderie of the female friendships around the hooking table.

Rose Fiumara is Corporate Account Executive for Eastern Computer in Knoxville. Tenn. She grew up in New York, moved to Atlanta, where she met her husband, Steve, and then moved to Norris Lake, near Knoxville. In her spare time, she likes to hook and spend time with her family.

Sandy Gannett, a St. Charles, Ill., resident, has been hooking since 1988, when she retired from full-time child advocacy work. Her art background and love of color and design led her to rug hooking, which has become her primary artistic focus. She has enjoyed creating pieces for herself and husband, their four adult children, and their families. She hooks mostly from her own designs. Sandy is a hooking teacher who works with Sue Hamer and likes learning from other teachers around the country.

Beverly Goodrich lives with her husband, Garth, on Lake Lanier in Gainesville, Ga. She has three grown daughters and three grandchildren. She has been hooking since 1992. She is also a folk art painter and likes to hook her own designs. Her work was also featured in *The Art of Rug Hooking*, and her hand-carved angels and Santas have been featured in such national magazines as *Victorian Christmas* and *Country Accents*.

Nancy Hackney lives with her husband, Mike, in South Boston, Virginia. She is a homemaker who loves antiques and folk art. She has two grown children, Eddie and Jennifer. Nancy has taught Jennifer to hook and the two do hooking demonstrations at the Prizery, a South Boston center to promote the arts.

Sue Hamer has been involved with textiles since she was a child, and is a knitter, quilter, and seamstress. (She was in charge of making the Illinois State Quilt, which is in the Executive Mansion in Springfield.) She started hooking rugs in 1973 with Leila Lindahl, a very inspirational teacher who at 91 is still teaching from her wheelchair in her home. Sue started her teacher training in 1983, became McGown-certified, and has been teaching ever since. When she was widowed after 35 years of marriage, with three children and three grandchildren, rug hooking became the major focus of her life. Now, she says, "the many friends and challenges hooking has brought to me have made it a total love affair."

Bryan Hancock started hooking in 1982, after admiring old hooked rugs that she couldn't afford. She lives in Rocky Mount, N.C., on a horse farm. She and her husband, Mike, and daughters, Catherine and Rebekah, live in a log home, which is a great setting for her hooked rugs.

Carol Houghton is a spiritual counselor, a Cherokee, a mother, wife, sister, and friend who believes that art is an expression of the movement of the divine through our lives and consciousness. She lives in Johnson City, Tenn.

Margaret Howell is a self-taught rug hooker. She hooked her first rug in 1935 without benefit of instructions, cutter, frame, or dyes. During World War II, she made four rugs, designing her own patterns and again cutting by hand, using recycled wool. She found a rug-hooking teacher in 1946, when she moved to Greenville, S.C., where she still resides. Margaret recalls Pearl McGown's coming to Greenville in 1948, approving Blyth Shoals as a rug camp, and bringing teachers from the North. Pearl and her sister set up a dyeing place on the front porch, with an oil stove. "It was great," says Margaret, who attended the first year and many more. She became a McGown teacher herself in 1964, and over the next 3½ decades has become a staple of workshops and rug camps, teaching, for example, for 25 years at Cedar Lakes and 18 at Old Salem. She also holds classes every week that she is at home.

Connie Hughes, from Sewickley, Penn., loves to "hook" people into rug hooking almost as much as she loves hooking rugs. She has been hooking for 10 years, and is a McGown teacher. She enjoys designing and hooking all rug-pattern genres from primitives to geometrics, florals, and pictorials.

Anna King is a folk-art potter, as is her daughter Crystal. Anna and her husband run Kings Pottery in historic Seagrove, N.C., the pottery capital of the world. Anna has been rug hooking for 10 years; she started under Jane King and Margaret Howell.

Rebecca Clark Knudsen graduated from Brigham Young University in 1975, with a B.A. in art and design. She worked in design in Provo, Utah. In 1976, she married Kurt Knudsen, with whom she has six children. They have lived in California and New Mexico, but have resided in her hometown of Provo since 1990. She is a self-taught rug hooker. Her rug hooking has been widely exhibited and has won numerous awards, including publication in three *Celebration of Hand-Hooked Rugs* books, published by *Rug Hooking* magazine.

Stephanie Krauss has been around rug hooking all her life. Her mother, Anne Ashworth, learned to hook when she was pregnant with Stephanie, so they've always joked about learning through osmosis. Stephanie and her siblings were raised on wool dust and dye fumes, so it was natural that she hook her first picture at age seven. It won a blue ribbon at the local fair. During her teenage years, Stephanie helped with her mom's custom-dyeing business and then started repairing rugs as a way to earn some extra money after the birth of her first daughter. She continues to repair rugs, but devotes most of her time to working with Green Mountain Rug School and Moxley Designs. Stephanie is currently establishing a small rug-hooking supply shop in Montpelier, Vt., where she lives with her three daughters.

Betty Laine lives in a suburb of Toronto, Ontario, Canada. She has two children and three grandchildren and has been a widow for ten years. Betty has been hooking for over 30 years and teaching for more than 20 years, mostly at rug camps.

Celia Leckerman, from Atlanta, Ga., began hooking rugs after seeing Mary Paul Wright and a rug she was hooking. Mary became Celia's teacher in 1986 and they have hooked through thirty or more rugs. Celia hand-cuts and dyes, overdyeing to make her rugs appear older than they are. As an art major and an interior designer, she sees this as her best work.

Gail Elizabeth Loder resides in the mountains of North Georgia with her husband and two daughters. Gail teaches visual arts at Rabun-Gap Nacoochee School, a private boarding school, where she also chairs the fine arts department. Gail has been hooking primitive rugs as a vehicle of self-expression for three years. Gail has a master's degree in education with certification in both art and home economics, along with a concentration in clothing and textiles. Rug hooking gives her an opportunity to use color and texture without fear of judgment or breaking rules. She finds it to be a very forgiving art form with inspiring results.

Mary Mann has a master's degree in higher education from American University; she taught mentally handicapped in public schools for 14 years. She was first introduced to rug hooking in New England in 1964 in an adult education class, but she began hooking in earnest under Naomi Stopher 20 years later. She now has Mary Williamson for a teacher. She is a member of the Bartow (Fla.) Art Guild, the Strawberry Hookers of Plant City, Fla. ("the strawberry capital of the world"), and ATHA. She is married with five children and four grandchildren.

Anne Mather, the author of *Creative Rug Hooking*, also wrote *The Art of Rug Hooking* and *Just for Today* (Harper San Francisco) and was co-author, with Louise Weldon, of *The Cat at the Door and Other Stories to Live By* (Hazelden) and its sequel, *The Cats in the Classroom*—books widely used in teaching and counseling. Anne also works as an editor for the Centers for Disease Control and Prevention. She lives with her husband, Brian Kelly, in Rabun Gap, Ga. They have two grown daughters, Maggie and Jeannie. Anne's work has been in numerous exhibits and is in many private collections. She does some commission work. Anne has a personal goal of getting every one of her seven brothers and sisters and their spouses to learn to hook. She's getting there....

Jane Mather hooked her first rug 3 years ago. She is a special education teacher in Raleigh, N.C. She lives there with her husband, Tom (an artist whose sketches are featured in *The Art of Rug Hooking* and *Creative Rug Hooking*), and their 10-year-old daughter, Emily, who also enjoys hooking.

John and Linda Mather live in Sautee Nacoochee, Ga., with their son, Nathaniel. They enjoy gardening and horses. Linda took up rug hooking 2 years ago—attending a class with her sister-in-law, Anne Mather, under Mary Williamson. John, an artist, draws up Linda's designs and, in the process, has gotten hooked himself. He has just completed his first rug.

Bett McLean attended the Memphis College of Art in the early seventies. For the next 19 years, she worked in graphic design, for a time as art director, for a publisher and a national media company. After converting to rug hooking, she began designing rugs. She lives with her daughter Hannah and husband, Doug Renfro, in Knoxville, Tenn. Her work was also featured in the *Art of Rug Hooking*.

Barbara Moran is a retired USAF lieutenant colonel; she served as an air evacuation nurse and counselor. A transplanted Rhode Islander, she lives in the North Georgia mountains. Her work has been widely exhibited, is in many private collections, and was featured in *The Art of Rug Hooking*.

Martha Morris, a mother of three and grandmother of four, lives in Gainesville, Ga., with her husband of over 55 years, William T. Morris, Jr. She has won national and international awards for her miniature portraits on ivory and recently an award for her book on genealogy. Rug hooking has been her favorite hobby since 1968. Her hooking was featured in *The Art of Rug Hooking*.

Patty Moskoff lives with her husband, George, and their four children outside of Chicago in Batavia, Ill. Patty began hooking rugs in 1996, when she saw her first hooked rug at a heritage festival. Since then, she has ventured out into dyeing wool and taking what she has learned from her teacher, Sue Hamer, and expanding to her own color combinations. When she is not hooking rugs, Patty works as a representative for a disease management company and helps her husband in the renovation of their home.

Sandy Myers lives in Gainesville, Ga., with her husband, Gary. Their son, Scott, and daughter-in-law, Rhonda, now live in Maryland. Sandy has been teaching quilting since the mid-'80s and her quilts have taken many awards on regional, state, and national levels. Her first rug, *Bethany Gardens*, was created under the guidance of Mary Williamson. The original design was taken from her miniature quilt, *Bethany Gardens*, the winner of numerous quilting awards. Sandy is now hooked on hooking.

Sarah Owens is retired after 30 years of teaching in America, the Bahamas, and Germany. She now lives in the North Georgia mountains.

Katie Puckett is the mother of two beautiful little girls—Judy, 4, and Marian, 2—as well as a full-time systems analyst for a major brokerage firm. Born and raised in Michigan, she and her husband, James, now live in Jacksonville, Fla. Both Katie's mother, Judy Colley, and grandmother, Marian Miller, were hookers, so rug hooking has been a part of her life "forever." She began her first rug in 1992. She is building up a hooking group in her area and also co-directs a new camp, begun in January 2000, in Jacksonville, called On the Ocean Rug School. She looks forward to the day when she can make her girls fourth-generation rug hookers.

Ruth Reenstra had two roosters (Howard and Corny) after whom the "chicks" in her rug *Vineyard Chicks* were colored. This is her first primitive in a wide-cut in 25 years of hooking.

Ruth is a wife, mother (three children), and grandmother (just one). She's lived in New Jersey, Indiana, Massachusetts, New Hampshire, and Pennsylvania, but now calls Summerfield, N.C., home. Her husband, son, and Ruth create folk-art lamps to sell retail (A Shade Different) and wholesale at gift markets.

Jan Robinson had always wanted to hook rugs. She was proficient in needlepoint and other textile arts. In 1992, she finally found Sue Hamer, her present teacher, and she has been hooking every day since then. Now a widow, Jan finds solace and relaxation in her hooking. She has finished many wonderful rugs from both dyed and as-is fabrics. Her family and friends are the lucky recipients of much of her beautiful work.

Mary Beth Robison graduated in 1978 from the College of St. Rose in New York with a B.S. in art education. She has lived in Atlanta since 1979 and manages Binders Art and Frame, a locally owned artists supply store. Her hobbies include designing and hooking rugs. *Parsley in the Lariope* was her first rug: she wanted something by which to remember her cherished friend, Parsley, who is now 15 years old.

Eric Sandberg, a costume supervisor in California for motion pictures such as *Jurassic Park, Pleasantville,* and *Hook,* had 25 years of needlework experience when he turned to rug hooking. His first rug was hooked following instructions that appeared in *Rug Hooking* magazine. When he finished the rug, it was then featured in the magazine. A certified McGown teacher, he has taught at the McGown Western Teachers Workshop in Oregon and at Caraway Rug School (Asheboro, N.C.). His rug *Africa's Gift* was a finalist in *Rug Hooking* magazine's Celebration IX and was voted Best of Show at the 1998 McGown Biennial Exhibit.

Dot Schutte has been rug hooking for over 30 years and has been a certified McGown teacher for much of that time. She lives and teaches classes in Gastonia, N.C., and has taught at several rug camps. She is serving now as assistant director of the Southeastern Teachers Workshop. She does some commission work.

Lois Sherwood, when not working on story rugs such as the *Pittsburgh Rug,* works around her farm in Pennsylvania. She has been hooking for about 10 years and is presently hooking her second story rug, depicting her mother's travel to Oklahoma in a covered wagon. Her third story rug will be about her John Deere tractors.

Phyllis Silverthorn moved to western North Carolina from the Atlanta area in 1994. She has a successful business as a massage therapist and bodyworker. She is a self-taught artist and enjoys using her creative imagination to design her rugs. She lives with her husband, Philip, two cats, three birds, and beloved mule in Scaly Mountain, N.C.

Pat Stolberg is an accredited McGown teacher and currently teaches an enthusiastic hooking group in Spring Hill, Fla. She learned to hook while living in Maine 34 years ago. When she retired from social work and moved to Florida, rug hooking became her full-time hobby. Her two adult daughters, one living in Maine and the other in Sitka, Alaska, are artists in other media.

Linda Stutz has been married 41 years; she has two children and seven grandchildren. She has been employed as an accounts receivable supervisor for 22 years. She has been enjoying traditional rug hooking for 23 years with Judy Colley as friend and teacher in Grand Rapids, Mich. She especially enjoys rug hooking at her cabin on Little Star Lake in Baldwin, Mich. Linda lovingly hooked her rug *Marie* with her black cocker spaniel Max as a model.

Patricia Tritt is an artist who graduated from San Diego State College; she also studied art at the University of Georgia; in San Miguel de Allende, Guanato, Mexico; and privately with noted artists. She paints in acrylic and watercolor. Her paintings have been exhibited and won awards in the Southeast, and she is a member of several art clubs and leagues. She turned her creative talents to rug hooking 12 years ago. Patricia designs most of her rugs and is a rug-hooking teacher. She and her husband, Bob, have lived in Georgia for 37 years. They now divide their time between Atlanta and Lake Rabun (Lakemont, Georgia).

Pam Wiegand, a graduate of Brenau College with a B.S. in nursing, began her fiber career in 1978 as an owner of and teacher at a needlework shop and fiber studio in Gainesville, Ga. She is an avid knitter, weaver, spinner, and rug hooker. She is an active member of the ATHA/Dogwood Rug Hooking Guild. She is currently working on her McGown teacher's certification. She teaches rug hooking in her studio and at John C. Campbell Folk School.

Mary Williamson is a retired dressmaker, sewing teacher, and mother of three. A McGown-certified teacher, she teaches in several rug camps annually, including Cedar Lakes (W. Va.), Caraway (N.C.), and Lazy Hills (Tex.). Her work is in many private collections. She now lives with her husband, Carey, in Clayton, Ga. When Naomi Stopher—founder of the Happy Hookers of Rabun County—died, Mary continued the tradition of teaching the local women to rug hook. *The Art of Rug Hooking* was dedicated to this wonderful teacher and her work was featured in it.

Faith Williston is a "Navy wife" who began traditional rug hooking in 1991 under the tutelage of Jacque Juvinal. Faith graduated in 1983 from Auburn University with a B.F.A. in painting; watercolors, tole, and acrylic painting had previously served as vehicles of her artistic expression. A number of her pieces have been chosen for display at the Naval War College Art Museum, and she has been featured in *Rug Hooking* magazine. She received her McGown certification in 1999.

Bitty Wisenbacker began hooking in 1987 under Mary Paul Wright. Bitty is a homemaker who lives with her husband in Marietta, Ga., and spends a lot of time in the mountains, on Lake Rabun. She has a son and daughter and three wonderful grandchildren.

Mary Paul Wright read an article in 1975 about rug-hooking lessons being taught through a parks department and immediately signed up. She knew she liked the country look, but seemed to be the only person in Atlanta who did, as she hooked alone for 10 years before discovering rug workshops—"What a joy!" Gradually, primitives became more popular, and she was asked to teach. She has 30 enthusiastic and talented students in the Atlanta area who now create some wonderful rugs. She feels rug hooking has brought her many hours of pleasure and wonderful friends.

Index

abrashing, 115
alphabets, 59–60, 138–139
Anderson, Lee, 102, 135, 140
Andreas, B.J., 26, 140
animals, hooking, 96–101
Armstrong, Jean, 45
Ashworth, Anne, 45
Association of Traditional
Hooking Artists (ATHA),
108, 122
Azeri™-style rugs, 110–111,
113, 115

Beatty, Alice, 45, 71
Becker, Patsy, 3, 33, 41, 56,
72–73, 104, 108, 132
Black, Elizabeth, 45
borders on house rugs, 106;
on orientals, 110; types of,
51–56
Bottjer, Marilyn, 40, 42,
81–82, 140
Brown, Barbara, 3. *See also*
Port Primitives.
Brubaker, Cherylyn, 132, 140
Bruce, Ethyl, 88
Buttler, Pris, 3, 24, 43, 45,
47, 57–63, 113, 118, 140

Callaway, Lib, 3, 45, 48, 50,
52–53, 55, 71–72, 134
Carroll, Barbara, 88
Chancey, Pat, 15, 140
Charco Patterns, 3, 4, 22, 26,
28, 64, 87, 89, 97,
110–112, 137
Charleson, Connie, 45
Cherokee "place of ease," 45
children, hooking, 83–95
child's art as pattern, 82, 96
Christmas stockings, 117
Clonts, Maryon, 20, 117, 140
Cole, Mary Lu, 104–105, 140
Colley, Judy, 19, 43, 45, 101,
140
color, 37–38, 40, 73; attic-
white, 70; marrying, 70,
75, 77; in orientals, 115;
removing, 75
cost-conscious tips, 77
Culberson, Marguerite, 18,
140
Cushing dyes, 71, 115; wools,
88
cutters, 121

Denlinger, Janet, 96, 141
DeRoos, Claire, 115
design, adapting, 43–56; sim-
plifying 43–45; story rug,

111, 113; tips, 56
DiFranza, Happy, 45, 47
directional hooking, 98, 106
doll clothes, 93–94, 130–131
dolls, 90, 118. *See also* **paper
doll rugs.**
DuVerger, Trudy, 17, 141
dyeing, by abrashing, 115;
details, 39; flesh tone formulas, 88; orientals, 115;
wools, 71, 106, 115

Evans, Mary, 53, 141
eyes, hooking, 88, 89, 97–98

faces, hooking, 87–89, 95
Findley, Nora, 103, 141
first rug, 17, 27, 38, 39, 51,
54, 74, 80, 81, 96, 99, 117,
141, 142, 143
Fiumara, Rose, 117, 141
Flynn, Jane McGown. *See*
Charco Patterns.
Fraser, Harry M., Co., 3, 42,
97, 102, 121, 135
fur/feathers, 98–99

Gannett, Sandy, 84–86, 88,
103, 141
Goodrich, Beverly, 56,
106–107, 141

Hackney, Nancy, 21, 141
Ham, Marion, **cover**, 85, 98,
104
Hamer, Sue, 3, 39, 40, 52,
64–67, 97, 99, 118, 125,
141
Hancock, Bryan, **cover**, 141
hand-cut wools, 73
Hieronimus, Ingrid, 111
hooker–stylists (featured),
Sue Hamer, 64, 65–67,
141; Rebecca Knudsen,
74–77, 141, Linda Mather,
68–70, 142; Martha
Morris, 71–73, 142
hooking, instructions,
120–121
Hornafius, Pat, 39, 102, 135
Houghton, Carol, 27, 45,
117, 141
houses, 102–107
Howell, Margaret, 4, 88, 141
Hughes, Connie, 111, 113,
141

King, Anna, 12, 41, 141
Knudsen, Rebecca Clark,
74–77, 84–86, 114, 141

Krauss, Stephanie,
108–109,141–142

Laine, Betty, 88–89, 110, 142
Lais, Emma Lou, 88
landscapes, 105
Leckerman, Celia, 98, 142
letting go, 78
lettering, 57–63
levels of hooking, 38–39
Little Quilts, 3, 118
Loder, Gail Elizabeth, 90–95,
128, 142

MacLennan, Nancy, 115
Mann, Mary, 8, 99, 142
marker bleed, 56
marrying wools, 70, 75, 77
Masters, Margaret, 32
Mather, Anne, 10, 13, 23,
30–31, 39, 41, 43–44, 52,
85, 87, 90–94, 99, 104,
117, 128, 142
Mather, Jane, 142
Mather, John, 51, 68, 142
Mather, Linda, **cover**, 68–70,
116–117, 133, 142
McGown, Pearl K., 9, 45
McLean, Bett, 3, 13, 23, 54,
136, 142
Merikallio, Patricia, 64
mistakes, 77
Moran, Barbara, 24, 33, 97,
142
Morris, Martha, 3, 16, 37, 43,
45–50, 52–53, 71–73, 98,
142
Morton House Primitives, 14,
52
Moshimer, Joan, 9, 45, 64,
78, 103
Moskoff, Patty, 14, 142
Myers, Sandy, 3, 80–81, 123,
142

Olsen, Jane, 88
oriental color scheme, 115
Owens, Sarah, 25, 36, 100,
142

paper doll rugs, 10, 90–94,
patterns, 128–131
patterns, changing, 43–50;
creating, 79–109, 122;
free, 123–139
Petruchik, Flo, 15
plaids, 55, 94
Port Primitives 3, 30–31, 41,
44, 133
prayer rugs, 74–77, 84, 86

Price, Charlotte, 3, 64, 113,
115
Pro-Chem dyes, 115
projects and patterns,
123–137
Puckett, Katie, 19, 101, 142

Rex, Stella Hay, 45, 68,
71–73
Reenstra, Ruth, 142–143
Robinson, Jan, 99, 143
Robison, Mary Beth, 99,
143
rug camps, 37
Rug Hooking magazine, 74,
140, 141, 143

sampler, 78
Sandberg, Eric, 28, 143
Santas, 118
Schutte, Dot, 22, 143
Sherwood, Lois, 113, 143
Siano, Margaret, 3
Silverthorn, Pyllis, 99–100,
143
sky, how to hook, 106
Smith, Jule Marie, 45, 64
Stolberg, Pat, 9, 143
stools, 117
story of a rug, *Bottom Star
—Big Dipper*, 108–109;
Scrap Cats, 101
story rug, 110–115
Stutz, Linda, 98, 143
style, 40–42
Sweet Briar Studio, 118
Szatkowski, Jeanette, 3

tote, 123–124
Townsend, Sharon, 78
Tritt, Patricia, 42, 82, 100,
106–107, 115, 118, 143
trivets, 125–127

Uncle Wiggily Classics, 18

vests, 116

Wiegand, Pam, 11, 60, 62,
143
Williamson, Mary, 3, 32, 45,
68, 70, 77, 89, 108, 116,
143
Williston, Faith, 111–112,
143
Wisenbacker, Bitty, 96, 143
Wright, Mary Paul, 29, 143
Yankee Peddler, 98

Yoder, Patty, 64